RENOVATING
THE
CHRISTIAN SOUL

RENOVATING THE CHRISTIAN SOUL

Kim Friend

© 2021 by Kim Friend

All rights reserved. No part of this book may be reproduced or transmitted in any form or by any means, electronic or mechanical, including photocopying, recording, or by any information storage and retrieval system, except in the case of brief quotations embodied in critical articles and reviews, without prior written permission of the publisher.

Although the author and publisher have made every effort to ensure the accuracy and completeness of information contained in this book, we assume no responsibility for errors, inaccuracies, omissions, or any inconsistency herein.

Unless otherwise noted Scriptures taken from the HOLY BIBLE, NEW INTERNATIONAL VERSION.® Copyright © 1973, 1978, 1984 by International Bible Society. Used by permission of Zondervan. All rights reserved.

Scriptures noted (NKJV) are taken from the New King James Version. Copyright © 1979, 1980, 1982, 1991 by Thomas Nelson, Inc. Used by permission. All rights reserved.

Scriptures noted (KJV) are taken from the *King James Version of the Bible*.

ISBN Paperback: 978-1-7345139-0-5
Library of Congress Control Number: 2020910388

Cover and Interior Design: Creative Publishing Book Design

Table of Contents

Chapter 1 — **R**elinquish	1
Chapter 2 — **E**xercise	21
Chapter 3 — **N**ot	57
Chapter 4 — **O**ne and Done	79
Chapter 5 — **V**ile	125
Chapter 6 — **A**ct	147
Chapter 7 — **T**rain	167
Chapter 8 — **E**valuate	207

CHAPTER ONE

Relinquish

*Certain traits are **Relinquished** that
sin might be extinguished.*

"I now pronounce you husband and wife. You may kiss the bride," I hear the preacher say. I am overwhelmed and excited with an abundance of joy, and it seems as if this moment is too wonderful to be real. I've waited for what seemed like an eternity for this very moment, and I'm thrilled beyond comprehension.

I was in eighth grade when I first began to notice him—I mean, *really* notice him. Oh, I'd seen him numerous times during the years before eighth grade, walking the halls of the middle school we both attended. He was always surrounded by other jocks in the school and the popular girls who loved his company simply because he was the most popular and kindest boy in school. He talked to everyone; he never excluded anyone for any reason, and he always wore a smile.

I am quite certain that if I had possessed the gumption to approach him or even glance his way from a distance of course, with a smile of my own, he would have happily returned one. But I was that student no one of his popularity status noticed. I was quite introverted, backwards and the teachers noticed me only because I was studious and always made school a priority.

It just so happened that he and I ended up in the same science class in our last year of middle school. On the first day of class, the teacher announced that we could choose where to sit and that would be our assigned seat for the year. Of course, the popular girls in the class waited to see where he sat first, each one earnestly hoping to beat all the other girls to the chair that sat empty beside him.

I took a seat in the front of the room as expected, but I was okay with that because every day for the next thirty-eight weeks I was going to be in the very same room with him. I was ecstatic that I would have the opportunity to see him longer than just the few moments it took to pass each other in the hallway. And upon entering that shared science class each day, my stomach would fill with butterflies.

I never did share with anyone my feelings about him. I didn't even know if butterflies in the stomach actually qualified as feelings. To be honest, I didn't really know exactly how I felt. I just knew I'd never thought about anyone like I thought about him. And I'm not sure if I thought about him because I was merely infatuated with his popularity and smile or because unfamiliar feelings were developing. And if the number of times I thought about him denoted more than casual feelings, then I definitely met that stipulation.

As the class progressed, one unit required that the entire class participate in an out-of-seat, hands-on experiment that was set up in stations and not necessarily in assigned groups. Some stations took longer which inevitably led to multiple students working the same station at times, and it just so happened that the timing worked in my favor as I ended up standing right beside him.

As we stood there, he took no real notice of me, though he did acknowledge my presence for the first time with that same smile he greeted everyone. As I was waiting for him to finish his part of the experiment, suddenly, without any prior thought or provocation, the words "I love you" fell from my tongue.

He turned quickly to face me, shocked to say the least and probably second-guessing if what he had just heard had really been spoken. As he looked at me, he might have even been scanning our station for some nearby person for whom that comment was truly intended. But as he looked around, he concluded that it was, in fact, just the two of us.

I was just as shocked. Taken aback even. But not nervous about what my tongue had just released. It wasn't as if I had to find the courage. Courage is something you gather purposely because you knowingly will be engaging in an event that necessitates it. I know it seems impossible, but the absolute truth is that I had no idea I was going to speak those words, let alone even speak to him. I never planned for those words to come out of my mouth. It had never even occurred to me that I had feelings like that for him. At that point, I hadn't definitively figured out why I thought of him so often.

As I remember those days, which after all this time are still so very vivid to me, I recognize how very much that particular relationship parallels my walk with Christ or, at one point, my lack thereof. Upon reflection, I can draw several parallels between the two.

- Just as that young man had taken no special notice of me up to that point, I took no notice of Christ in my daily living.
- Just as no courage was required to say "I love you" to him, no courage is required to speak with Jesus.
- Just as I never shared my so-called feelings about this boy with others, I never shared anything with Jesus.

- Just as my spoken "I love you" altered the course of our soon-to-be relationship forever, Jesus intends for our salvation to be a forever life-changing, life-altering occurrence.

I did not purposely neglect to engage with Jesus. I can honestly say that I just never thought of Christ in terms of relationship. But why didn't I think of Him in those terms? He is my Heavenly Father. I work so faithfully and earnestly to maintain earthly relationships with those I dearly love. Why hadn't I done the same with Jesus?

Did I not think in terms of relationship because Jesus was not physically before me day in and day out? Was it because I didn't love Him? And how could that be? He gave His life for me that I might have life (See John 10:10.) How could I not love someone that considers my very soul of such worth that the God of Heaven hung on an old rugged cross for it? The worth of my soul is so great to God that I cannot begin to comprehend it.

If and when we begin to mull over such questions, it is at this point that we must seriously consider a renovation—a renovation of our souls. In order for any renovation to begin, we must first acknowledge the need for it. Sometimes concluding that we need renovation is by far the hardest part. But when we finally recognize the error of our ways, we must delve into the much-needed change faithfully, never pulling back because it becomes too hard or seems impossible. We must remember that with Christ all things are possible, the most important of which is the renovation of our soul.

I Will Relinquish

Those three words—"I love you"—spoken to that young boy during class paved the course of my entire life. Three words can forever change our course in our walk with Christ. They are simply, "I will relinquish…"

The day we decided that we needed to be forgiven, for whatever reason, should have been the very same day we understood the need to relinquish those things in our lives for which we had just sought forgiveness. But for some reason forgiveness and relinquishment never happen simultaneously. It might be the case that whatever we need to relinquish will require a process. Being forgiven should encourage us to initiate the relinquishment.

As in life, what we seek to either put aside, surrender or give up requires us to forfeit some part of our lives or even some part of ourselves in order to maintain that which we have relinquished.

It's never too late to initiate change. It is always worth taking the risk to leave behind who we were to take on the challenge of who we can become. You may be the person who gave his life to Christ thirty years ago, still wondering why nothing is different in your life as a result of having been saved. Or maybe there was a change, but it was short-lived.

Is it possible that there was no change because we deceived ourselves into thinking this change would be automatic and nothing would be required of us for this change to occur? Perhaps, during the course of both the sermon and the altar call, we misunderstood that change would somehow synchronously happen the moment we spoke *will you forgive me.* Or is it that we did in fact understand that change must begin with us and so we attempted to surrender some things in our lives, with or without the help of Christ, but the change we sought was never permanent?

Hopefully at some point after our salvation even if misunderstandings did occur, we gained the knowledge that we no longer live for ourselves. "And he died for all, that those who live should no longer live for themselves but for him who died for them and was raised again" (2 Corinthians 5:15). In order that we may live for Him, let us consider the parts of our lives or even ourselves that we can voluntarily relinquish that will aid us in living a life for Christ.

Old Habits

Why does it seem so much easier to set a New Year's resolution for weight loss than it does to live a life committed to Christ? Essentially, they both require a lifelong commitment, they both require that the "relinquish initiator" is us, and they both require assistance to attain the end result.

We long to relinquish, shed or cast off the weight. Weight loss is pursued because people long to change something about themselves, whether it be appearance, energy levels or overall health. We begin by deciding to join a weight loss program. Part of the program includes specially formulated foods that contain fewer calories and less salt, or perhaps a wellness coach to aid in battling the periodic temptation to unnecessarily indulge in food. Lastly, an obvious part of any weight loss program is to incorporate a daily exercise regimen.

Unfortunately, a commitment to weight loss far outlasts a commitment to Christ. And that begs the question of how many people really continue on a weight loss program *for life*? At least for the time we choose to remain committed to it, our continued dedication may be solely due to the physical change we notice over a short period of time. When our progress is recognized, not only by us in numbers on the scale but also by others as they notice the physical changes and praise us for our dedication and effort, the recognition motivates us to keep plowing through. With weight loss, we can justifiably be our own cheerleader as well as welcome the cheers of those around us who see our progress.

However, when we fail Jesus, sometimes it's difficult to cheer ourselves on and remain uplifted. And we certainly do not have outside cheerleaders praising us every time we make a godly, obedient choice during the course of our day. In fact, it's usually the case that no one else sees our life of obedience unto Him which is a good thing because had they recognized it, chances are we did something for all to see that fell outside biblical parameters. Sometimes we begin to keep count like we do with our weight loss, the number of times we've maintained obedience versus the number of times we've failed. Eventually, overwhelmed by our failure, we throw in the towel.

The Christian life is a lot like a weight loss life. One day we decide to join Jesus Christ's program. Just as we desire to change something about ourselves in a weight loss program, we have that same desire to change something in our lives when we join Jesus' program. Perhaps we cannot bear the burden of life on our own any longer. Maybe our attempts to handle life's circumstances have been unsuccessful, serving only to make our burden heavier and even more unmanageable. Maybe we feel a need to be loved by Christ, knowing that *His* love for us never wavers.

As with any program, a process of implementing the program steps and directives is necessary to help ensure success. The first part of God's program is His very own specially formulated food—the Word of God. He is the accountability partner needed to aid in times of temptation and weakness. And just like daily exercise is a must, an obvious part of God's regimen must be daily prayer and communication with Jesus.

Old habits die hard. In order that we rid ourselves of unwanted habits in our lives, a concentrated, forced effort (at first) must be made. In time, the forced effort that we initially put forth will transform into a genuine longing. Some of the old habits that we will need to kick to the curb to ensure success in God's program include…

"I" Statements

For some reason, Christian living seems to be the most difficult concept for us to take hold of and *keep* hold of. Our efforts seem short-lived. Perhaps it is because the benefits of chucking certain things in our lives in order to live for Christ are not seen soon enough or maybe we seek benefits that are unrealistic and illogical. It could be that the understanding that our lives are no longer our own was missed altogether the moment we were saved. Maybe some thought it was optional for our lives to no longer be our own. Those who view life after salvation as a mere continuance of all that we *currently* are and do, don't recognize God's precepts that are to be fully obeyed (See

Psalm 119:4), consequently, not requiring Christ daily for the strength needed to obediently implement these precepts.

"And he died for all, that those who live should *no longer* live for *themselves* but *for him* who died for them and was raised again" (2 Corinthians 5:15, author emphasis). This isn't suggestive of suddenly quitting a day job to become a missionary and travel the globe, nor does it suggest keeping your day job while signing up for night school to study to become a theologian. It doesn't mean that every moment we live and breathe should be spent fasting and praying, unless of course, you feel led by the Holy Spirit to do any of these things mentioned above.

But for those of us that long for *Christ's* will and guidance in our daily living, a habit to relinquish from the start are those "I" statements that consume our daily thoughts. These sentences usually sound like "What should I…," "Will I…," or "How will I…." If these sentences are a common occurrence in our vocabulary, they do not reflect a need for or focus on Christ daily in our lives.

Relinquishing the "I" statements in our lives is a part of no longer living for ourselves. The thoughts we have concerning the paths we take, the choices we make and those with whom we surround ourselves should be evolving into questions that shift the focus from ourselves to God. The questions concerning our lives would sound more like:

"Is this God's will for my life," or "Will the choices I make glorify God?" These should be the questions that serve to steer and guide us in living Christ daily.

Good Choices

Our lives are the choices we make. As we begin to relinquish the "I" statements in our lives and replace them with the "God" statements, it would be a natural progression then that we move from the good choices we made to the godly choices we make.

The choices we make never affect only us, the choice maker. Regardless of how insignificant the choice may seem; it always affects other people. Even in something so trivial as deciding to get a haircut, others are affected. Children may need a sitter, a ride may be needed to and from the barber, or plans might need to be changed altogether during the course of the week so as to make it to the shop when it's actually open.

Our choices can impact the lives of those around us, even outside of our family circle—those we know, and those we don't know. Our choices can affect others in a positive or negative way. They can be lifelong, short-lived, life-shattering, or a lifelong blessing. The choices we make sometimes affect the entirety of our life or even the entirety of someone else's. With choices owning such impact and power, it seems imperative that we make every attempt possible to make choices that cause either very little or even no disruption to the lives of others. Let's relinquish good choices and choose to make godly choices.

Personally, I had never given thought to godly choices. I thought of choices only in terms of good or bad, but not godly. As my children grew older, especially when they began to drive, my husband and I became less and less privy to all that might be happening in their lives. I began to realize that one of my most fervent prayers was that Christ would help my children make good choices in our absence.

As that prayer continued, all too soon those very words, *God help my children to make good choices,* were more correctly spoken by the Holy Spirit (See 1 Corinthians 2:13.) The spiritual truth was to ask God to help my children make *godly* choices.

In my Christian immaturity, while simultaneously and unwisely relying solely on my human knowledge, I began to think, *Well, Lord, isn't a good choice equivalent to a godly choice?* That question unleashed a geyser of examples that proved otherwise. Not only did I begin to learn the momentous difference in making a good choice versus a godly choice, I also began to learn to always incorporate divine knowledge, first and foremost, when attempting to shed light on anything spiritual. Over time, the Holy

Spirit began to reveal to me examples of good choices versus godly choices. These examples specifically concerned my own children—godly choices, I prayed fervently, for them to live in their own lives.

A Good Choice	*A Godly Choice*
Protected sex before marriage	Abstinence before marriage
Let's drink, but not drive	Don't drink
Don't laugh when the crowd you're in pokes fun at someone	Speak up on behalf of the one being made fun of
Stopping off with friends, just for a few minutes, at a house your parents asked you not to go to	Drop off your friends and return home

The Lord wants our focus to ever remain on Him that we might make godly choices. He aids us in rerouting our thought focus from human to divine. It is inevitable that when we make a godly choice versus a good choice, the godly choice causes little, if any, disruption to our own life or the lives of those around us. Our godly choices are the guaranteed determinant to living a shameless and regretless life, one hundred percent of the time, while glorifying Him.

Being Content

Being content most often births a positive feeling. And it certainly can if we've taken every precaution to exceed in life. Most of us would define being content in life as wanting or needing no more or being pleased and happy right where we are.

But being content in life can be negative when it causes stagnation. Those who live this negative contentment include those who are unmoved, satisfied, comfortable and unconcerned about where they are currently or even regarding where they may be headed in life. This type of contentment leaves no room for growth, hope or aspiration to be more than who or what we are right now at this time in our lives. If we are just as content today, as the day we decided we needed Christ, we've chosen to live a content and idle life for Jesus; we are satisfied, comfortable, and unconcerned about what our salvation was supposed to do in our lives. We live this negative contentment. Initially, the day we were saved was the day we decided that we wanted to be so much more than a tally mark in the "I'm saved" box. We wanted to be more than the church's need to keep track of the number of people who commit their lives to Christ. We decided the day we were saved that our lives would be different.

In the beginning, being forgiven felt good. We experienced incredible relief the moment we were forgiven for our sins—all our sins. We realized our sins were nailed to that cross where Jesus hung. We decided to commence upon a new journey in hopes of great change; a decision that was made with great excitement and anticipation. Goals were set; goals that were initially intended to last a lifetime: daily Bible reading, daily communion with Christ, and daily obedience.

But what happened to the journey on which we were so excited to embark? When did this negative contentment settle into our lives as Christians? Was it that life seemed to get in the way or that spending time with friends began to take priority in our lives? Or maybe it was as simple as being too tired after the day had run its course. We told ourselves in the beginning we'd live a lifelong commitment to Christ. And in this lifelong commitment, we'd glorify Him while living the promises of God. However, we alone, are responsible for having made the decision to allow that pledge to fall by the wayside.

We meander in and out of the life of Jesus. If we've stopped our daily regimen with Him, we tell ourselves repeatedly that we'll catch up tomorrow on Bible reading and pray longer another day. Ultimately, we find ourselves actually living that tally mark in the "I'm saved" box. Our lives reflect no growth, no hope, no new aspirations. We have fallen into living a negative contentedly saved life.

Imagine being in a loving, committed relationship, one in which there is an abundance of conversation and time devoted to one another. That togetherness is what solidifies the relationship and allows it to flourish.

Now imagine over time, for whatever reason, the conversations lessen as does the time spent together. You notice it happening but think it will get better. You force yourself to believe that you're going through a temporary dry spell in the relationship. But all the while you're going through this dry spell, your relationship is suffering.

The same thing happens with Jesus, but the monumental difference is that Jesus is so much easier to set aside than the situations and people in our lives. Because we can physically see people and meet situations, we are forced to confront them daily. As we spend less and less time in the things of Christ, feelings of guilt may emerge. But all too soon that guilt subsides because we are so easily able to fill our lives with something else.

If we allow ourselves to remain content, unmoved, and satisfied in our salvation, we become much like a retention pond. We've all seen retention ponds. They're everywhere as they are a created must. Over time, the pond fills with rainwater. Some ponds are equipped with fountains, but others are not. Without a fountain, the water lies motionless and unstirred. In time, that stagnant water produces a foul odor. But if the pond is equipped with a fountain, the fountain moves the water day after day thus preventing stagnation and foul odor. Additionally, perpetual use of the fountain helps to inhibit the growth of algae and bacteria, which enhances the water quality.

Our lives as Christians can potentially mimic that of a retention pond:

We are the pond. And the day we accepted Christ, as He is the living water (See Jeremiah 17:13, NKJV.), we were filled. As we remain eager participants in walking as Jesus did, the fountain of living water remains active and in motion. But the moment we choose to go idle in our walk, the fountain goes idle. Jesus will not force the fountain to run. *We* are responsible for maintaining the working order of the fountain.

In choosing to remain motionless and idle in our walk, we automatically engender a spiritual lifelessness. As a result, a foul odor sets in caused by the algae and bacteria of sin. In our choice to cast off this negative contentment whereby we were satisfied, comfortable and unconcerned about our current representation of our salvation, we flip the fountain back on, thus causing the fountain of living water to flow once again. The flowing of this living water promotes new growth, new hope, and new aspirations.

This fountain is the very necessary sustenance of life by which all spiritual life is fed. Inevitably, as a fountain enhances water quality in a retention pond, Jesus Christ as the fountain of living water in our lives will do no less than to improve the quality of our spiritual lives.

CHAPTER TWO

Exercise

*The wise **Exercise**.*

A Child Saved

I have been saved since the age of nine. I remember it like it was yesterday: where it happened, who led me to Christ, and the brand-new Bible I received. It was my first one ever. I cherished it. The gift of it made me feel proud, as if *I* had accomplished something. But that's the mindset of a child—unable to grasp that *I* had accomplished nothing, and instead, Jesus had done it for me.

As a child, I spent the majority of my time outdoors, weather permitting. I absolutely craved exploring the neighborhood on my yellow bike equipped with the fancy banana seat and adorned with an oversized basket made of inexpensive, brilliant white plastic with flowers affixed to the front for all to see as I pedaled along the sidewalks. The handlebars also displayed multi-colored tassels hanging from the rubber grips. And of course, my wheel spokes sported striped, straw-like attachments that played a repeating *clickety–click* sound as the wheels turned on the concrete pavement.

I quite enjoyed riding my bike to the house of a friend my age, who lived down the street and around the corner. We often played cards and board games on her front porch, and I sometimes enjoyed a lunch with her that was comprised of the famous peanut butter and jelly sandwich accompanied by cheese cubes and a juice drink.

One afternoon as her mom made her way to the front porch with our lunches, she stopped to talk with me. She invited me to a get-together called Vacation Bible School. She held the event in her garage. I remember telling her I'd never heard of Vacation Bible School and asked her what it was. She replied that many children attended to learn about Jesus through songs and stories.

On the last day of Bible school, she asked me to sit with her away from the other children. I remember her telling me how very much Jesus loved me and that He died for me. I cannot remember her speaking the actual term sin or even speaking of the blood Jesus shed on the cross. Perhaps she thought because of my youth, I would be overwhelmed by trying to understand sin, or that I would not comprehend the significance of Christ's shed blood.

She began to tell me about heaven, but she never discussed death as preceding one's entrance into heaven. I don't recall her talking about the concept of eternity. What I do recall, vividly, is her describing to me that there is a door to my heart. She told me Jesus was standing at the door to my heart knocking, as she fashioned her hand into a fist and knocked at the invisible door in midair. She then asked me if I would open the door to allow Him to come into my heart, to live and to love me all the days of my life.

Excitedly, and with no hesitation, I responded with an emphatic *yes*. I cannot be sure why I was in fact so excited. But I do know that I felt joy, though as a child, I would not have chosen that word at the time to describe how I felt.

Though I didn't fully realize it then, from that day forward, my life would be forever changed. As a child, I could not possibly give purposeful thought to the way I lived my newly converted life. I was nine. My days were filled with thoughts of making sure I had enough time to return to my adventuresome bike riding and playing outdoors with friends. And sadly, even in most of my adult life, though I was converted, I gave no purposeful thought to how I lived outwardly as a Christian. Though I did, with great effort, try to do the "right thing"—whatever the right thing seemed to be according to how *I* defined right, as opposed to how God defined "right." I now realize that doing the right thing is a human endeavor while doing the godly thing is a spiritual endeavor.

Today, my life is filled with much spiritual exercise—exercise that I greatly anticipate. Committed exercise to which I now give purposeful thought because I know as we all do that exercise performed with pertinacity reaps incredible benefits in our lives.

Exercise Validation

Be careful, however, that the exercise of your freedom does not become a stumbling block to the weak. – 1 Corinthians 8:9

Setting an Example

This Scripture creates an image for me that cannot easily be forgotten. Every stumbling block causes harm, which is certain to produce a wound—whether physical or psychological, seen or unseen, temporary or lifelong. Sometimes these wounds can comprise any number of these simultaneously with the potential to scar for life. The stumbling block itself is only *indirectly* responsible for the wound incurred. As Christians, practicing or not, *we* are *directly* responsible for launching this stumbling block. We plant this stumbling block knowingly or unknowingly, and

Exercise

in doing it unknowingly, we are no less accountable for the wound it produces.

The stumbling block is interpreted as anything that contradicts the Word of God. It can be seen, heard or both by the saved and the unsaved alike. It is usually evidenced in one of three manifestations but can conceivably be witnessed in all three. As Christians, the words we speak, the choices we make and the lives we lead can, in an instant, knowingly or unknowingly, serve as the stumbling block in another's life.

As Christians, we are all guilty, no one excluded, at some point or even currently of behavior that has been a stumbling block in the life of someone else simply because we are imperfect human beings. Teachers, pastors, neighbors, co-workers, husbands, wives, moms and dads are all guilty of committing stumbling block character at one time or another.

Because we as Christians are held to a higher standard than those who are not, *our* mistakes are identified as stumbling blocks. The unsaved person's mistakes are simply just mistakes, not committed with harmful intent toward the innocent. But in God's eyes, we as Christians must be attentive to our actions. We deceivingly tell ourselves that our choices, our words and our lives don't impact others, especially in regards to salvation. We support this notion by entertaining the idea that people are individuals making their own choices and leading their own lives not predicated upon what *others* say and do.

In actuality, a greater number of people probably choose conformity to feel accepted thereby fostering feelings of questionable self-esteem and worthiness. As Christians, we neglect to grasp the verity of how much more our lives are closely monitored, investigated and scrutinized by others—as they should be. In choosing to be a Christian, we have a standard to uphold—the standard of emulating Christ in our lives. This emulation is our validation that we are Christians.

Everything we do and say can tremendously and profoundly impact those around us. Even among the unsaved, the things we do and say can be reasons for them to decline salvation altogether. Though their choice, we can be responsible for having inflicted this potentially irreversible wound—declining salvation altogether. Our choices can serve as the stumbling block to others. It is possible for a Christian to drive an unbeliever to the conclusion that Christianity is a life of hypocrisy and as a result they choose not to partake in what they consider to be a pretense. On the other hand, saved individuals may begin to interpret our poor lifestyle choices as acceptable in the eyes of Christ. Such deception leads to diminished godly choices, which in turn leads to a life *independent* of Jesus. This inflicts a wound that scars for life.

Exercise Representation

In what greater capacity should we set the bar in becoming the example that is not a stumbling block? It is in fact as parents. The home provides the ultimate foundation upon which our children grow. It is here that children learn that honesty is promoted, forgiveness is practiced, love is determined and salvation is birthed. It is here that self-esteem and worthiness are gained. Our children become the teachers, the pastors, the neighbors, the co-workers, the husbands, the wives, and the moms and dads of tomorrow.

We are our children's teachers. And as such, Paul says, "Not many of you should presume to be teachers, my brothers, because you know that we who teach will be judged more strictly" (James 3:1). As Christians who choose to become parents, we serve in the fundamental capacity of biblical teachers whose primary responsibility is not only the introduction of but also the continuation of God's precepts into the lives of our children. As we live them, we teach them. And in rearing children, the home is the crucial foundation that provides the environment that is conducive to nurturing a well-adjusted, abundantly loved and self-confident child. In that apparent understanding, all that we say and do before our children becomes a lesson learned. Ultimately, our lives should be a representation of our salvation, an emulation of Jesus Christ.

Shortly after my husband and I were married, we longed to start a family. After much fertility treatment and surgery, we were finally able to conceive. I often thought to myself: *My children will have a wonderful life. They will be much loved by both parents, and we will set a good example for them by which to live.*

But in discovering the stumbling-block Scripture, a revelation unfolded—*I* was a stumbling block, and worse yet, to those who meant the most to me—my children. I cannot know the souls I adversely affected because of my choices. Most of my life did not align with the Word of God. I certainly did not lead a Christian lifestyle by example, and my children witnessed this the most. In not living a representation of my salvation, I failed to take advantage of ways to institute a lifestyle that witnessed my love for Jesus. When tucking them into bed at night, I failed to engage in prayer with them. Though we memorized weekly Bible verses, I didn't explain to my children, in a childlike instruction, how these Bible verses applied to our own lives.

But in so many more important ways, virtuous ways, I failed at setting a godly example. I failed to exemplify godly traits such as forgiveness, patience, self-control and

Exercise

pardon. When I chose to argue with my husband in front of my children, I failed to demonstrate self-control. In walking away angry, I failed to demonstrate pardon. When I chose to go without speaking to my husband, still mad from the day before, I failed to demonstrate forgiveness. When I honked at someone for not driving how I thought they should be driving, I failed to demonstrate patience.

As Christians, we should live these virtues as though they were woven into the very fiber of our being, thereby becoming the indispensable example by which our children learn. As our children witness this pattern of response, they will instinctively begin to employ these learned, powerful virtues as their own responses in daily living. It is hopeful then that these intrinsic virtues can secure less probability of being a stumbling block in the lives of others.

The words "to the weak" suggest that those who become the victims of a stumbling block are weak in Christ in some way. But can the magnitude of the Scripture lie in grasping the revelation that those responsible for causing the stumbling block are themselves the weakest of all? The weakness of the individual lies in the mere "claim" to be a Christian while living in a way that doesn't mirror Christianity.

Anyone can claim to be anything at any time. Take for example the individual drafted into the NFL or the MLB. After his career has ended, he can claim to have been a great athlete, but his career stats can confirm his claim or substantiate the complete opposite.

The same holds true for Christians. We can lay claim to being a Christian, but do our lives reflect what we are asserting? At the end of our Christian "career" what will our "career stats" corroborate? Will they prove that our lives emulated Christ by living His guiding precepts? Or will they verify that the only reason our Bibles aren't camouflaged with dust is because we carry them to church every now and again? Our eternal hope is not secured by our regular church attendance, nor is it secured by our church titles such as church elder, choir singer, piano player or Sunday school teacher. Let us not be counted among those who will live the proven conclusion—just because we show up doesn't mean we're going up (See Romans 2:13.)

It is hopeful that in our longing to live obediently because of our love for Jesus, we are suddenly now acutely aware of our surroundings and those who occupy them. Our focus should become the eternity of each individual's soul. In exercising the combination of living God's precepts and focusing on the salvation of others, our lives should be such that we are mindful to avoid being a stumbling block. Though we make a conscious effort, as humans we will fail. But when we do, we recognize our failure, repent for it, and refuse to repeat what led us to repent.

Exercise

There is never a deadline exceeded whereby forgiveness is not granted. And in the delay to seek forgiveness, once sought, hasn't expired. I know that children are impressionable. And I know it would be easy for my children to recall the not-so-good choices—the stumbling block episodes—they've witnessed in me at certain points in my life. But as long as we live and breathe, it is never too late to begin a renovation of our souls. It is never too late to be forgiven and actually live a life that reflects our Christianity without having to verbalize that we are, in fact, Christians.

Exercise Prayer

The effective, fervent prayer of a righteous man avails much.
– James 5:16, NKJV

Lesson Learned

Communication is and should be the pivotal foundation upon which all relationships build and grow. It is solely in prayer that we begin to establish a relationship with Jesus. His Word alone encompasses the godly principles by which we are to live. But it is only through the power of prayer in communication with Him that we are enabled to sow these precepts into our daily lives. It is the combination of Scripture and prayer that permits the revelation of all that God desires for our lives. Because everyone is unique, this communication is mandatory as it permits the divine revelation of a much-needed change that is exclusive to each of us.

In our relationships, we often disclose unknown information about ourselves to one another. Such divulgence could possibly stir feelings of guilt, shame, distrust, weakness and insecurity not only in us, but possibly in the person with whom we're sharing our delicate, handle-with-care personals. But because God already knows us better than we know ourselves, we can feel comfortable sharing anything with Him. In fact, we often gain a peace in doing so.

In general, as Christians, we share a communal responsibility to emulate Jesus, as God desires for our lives. No revelation was necessary to know to live such responsibility. We know for example to live such virtues as honesty, compassion and forgiveness. Unbelievers know to live these as well. The worthy difference between both sets of people living such character is to whom the honor and glory go in the completion of living such traits. In the life of a believer, all that we live in a life that walks as Jesus did, the honor and glory in the fulfillment of such goes to Jesus Christ.

But as Christian individuals and not as a Christian community, there can be divine revelation that is specific to that individual. The change needed as divulged in the revelation given by the Holy Spirit is particularly essential.

Exercise

When very specific revelation is given, we know it is a necessity that we must seek to live as these very changes become the building block required to move us into the next longing of God for our lives; be it a new discernment, a new lesson, a new understanding or even another new revelation. All used and intended by God for spiritual growth.

It was through prayer that the Holy Spirit began to reveal to me that *I* was a stumbling block in the lives of others (See 1 Corinthians 8:9.) Of course, part of my prayer time is spent on routinely lifting up my children before the face of the Lord. In doing so, the Spirit began to cause me to think about my actions before my children and those who know me. Both sets of people are aware that I am a believer.

I began to ask myself how many times those people have seen me at my worst? And when I've been at my worst, wherever I may have been, who else was there to witness my words or actions? How many of them were saved? How many of them were unsaved? In times past that was no concern of mine.

But of the saved individuals who knew me, I began to wonder if they sometimes shook their heads in disappointment or even thought to themselves, *We'll have to add her to our prayer list.* They certainly had every right to do so. The words *I'm saved* should align with our choices as well as our choice of words.

And what about those who were not saved? Did I convince them that because we're Christians absolutely anything we say and do is acceptable to Jesus as long as we ask to be forgiven later? If so, they were more than likely asking when and where they could sign up to become a Christian. Maybe some thought the opposite: *Boy, she is a hypocrite. She is exactly the reason I will never become a Christian.*

At that time in my life, the choices I made and the words I spoke made me fully responsible for stirring undesirable emotions in the hearts and minds of those who surrounded me. At that time, I was not aware of the damage I was causing to their souls, but I was and still am responsible for conducting myself in a manner worthy of the gospel of Christ (See Philippians 1:27.) Yet, I had done nothing of the sort. God needed me to take hold of that responsibility and ask to be forgiven. Prayer is the only conduit through which these imperative revelations unfold.

Prayer is the one thing, the only thing, from which nothing bad stems. When we yield to His guidance revealed in prayer, it is guaranteed to beget only wonderful results in the lives of those who are avidly seeking the face of God. As a result of the revelation that I was a stumbling block, only prayer and a willing heart could commence change.

Though I know, once asked to be forgiven it is granted, my heart continued to break as I was being disciplined

Exercise

(See Hebrews 12:11.) We know this discipline all too well because we continue to feel unforgiven though we know *that* to be in direct opposition to what Christ did at the cross. What I expected innocently enough was that I'd ask to be forgiven and I would suddenly feel guiltless, fully aware not to repeat the offense. However, the discipline encouraged a necessary, heartfelt growth and it happened because of the fervent prayer of a righteous man. When we come before Christ with a *willing* heart, amazing things begin to happen. A much-needed transformation begins to emerge. And this change, once achieved, is liberating to us and glorifying to Christ.

I longed for that change. It crushed me when the Lord revealed to me that I had served as a stumbling block to many but mostly my own children. But I also realized that His will for me was to know "my son, do not despise the chastening of the Lord, nor be discouraged when you are rebuked by Him; for whom the Lord loves He chastens" (Hebrews 12:5-6, NKJV).

Only in this prayer pursuit as part of the renovation of my soul did I come to understand that, as a result of fervent prayer, Christ longs to stamp upon our hearts indelible, godly lessons. This transformation avails much as it causes effective living for Him. He wants us to comprehend that in all we do, consciously or subconsciously, it always, always,

always affects those who surround us. No man lives to himself. Our actions and our words affect the heart and mind of others as well as ourselves. And they do so with greater magnitude because we carry the title of *Christian*.

We inherited this title the moment we were saved. While this inheritance would have no value when drawn up in an earthly will, it is spiritually priceless. However, with any title comes responsibility. Some titles bear much more responsibility than others and with some titles that responsibility is not just to a select few but to a multitude of people. And so it is with being a Christian.

The most meaningful, significant title anyone can possess is that of *Christian*. In my spiritual immaturity, I assumed this responsibility only concerned me. I never gave thought to how my actions or even the lack thereof could cause detriment to another's soul, as well as my own. To know that my actions, my words and my choices could potentially corrupt the very soul of another human being was heart-wrenching to me. Even if in all I did, somehow miraculously, no one was negatively affected, I am filled with remorse knowing I evoked feelings of great sorrow in my Heavenly Father. He provides us the privilege of having His name stamped upon our lives and our hearts, and He offers us the gift of eternal salvation. In return, our lives should at the very least, yield a representation of gratitude by emulating Him.

Exercise

We must make it our aim "do not cause anyone to stumble, whether Jews, Greeks or the church of God—even as I try to please everybody in every way. For I am not seeking my own good but the good of many, so that they may be saved. Follow my example, as I follow the example of Christ" (1 Corinthians 10:32-11:1). If we are ever mindful of living the example that Christ intends, it is expected that we will not purposely mislead anyone, saved or otherwise. Our lives lived should be such an expression of Jesus Christ that we become a most powerful walking testimony of our ever-resolute faith and steadfast loyalty to Jesus Christ without the requirement of spoken words as to the testament of such.

Exercise Getting to Know Jesus Christ

Now this is eternal life: that they may know you, the only true God, and Jesus Christ, whom you have sent. – John 17:3

Presumption

The one that filled my stomach with butterflies in science class that I mentioned in Chapter 1 presumed to know me, though his only source of reference included my outward appearance, my introversion and what he had heard through the grapevine. And if he had categorized me, he would have chosen the "nerd" classification. We're all too familiar with this category, whether we ourselves lived this classification or merely viewed it from the outside. It's the category that absolutely no one purposely struggles to become a part of. Somehow, regrettably, once branded with this stigma, which is cruel at best, we carry it for an undetermined length of time—perhaps all our school days and even after we graduate. And though this was not a term he was responsible for having coined, the popular guys in school were proficient in classifying all their peers into one of two categories—*popular* or *nerd*.

In actuality, this popular boy knew nothing about me. He knew nothing about my character, my principles, or my virtue. But he couldn't know them; he'd never communicated with me. I was okay with that. I never had any intention of meeting him, primarily because I knew that the possibility of us meeting was implausible. But it turned out that I was wrong. We both ended up attending a year-end party given by one of our few mutual acquaintances in middle school. I would have never guessed that my very small circle of friends somehow slightly overlapped his very large group of popular friends.

When we were finally, and legitimately, introduced at this party by a football player who happened to be my neighbor, I was suddenly nervous. Nervousness was a feeling I'd never experienced before when I passed him in the hallway or even during the incident in science class. I couldn't help but wonder if my nervousness was somehow being misinterpreted as embarrassment because the opportune time had unlikely presented itself for him to pursue the question why I had told him I loved him. I'm quite sure any response would have been unreasonable and illogical in his opinion. I certainly could have spoken the truth, attempting to explain to him who the Holy Spirit is and how He works in the lives of those who are saved. He would undeniably have perceived this as nonsense and without hesitation withdrawn me from the *nerd* category and immediately placed me in the *insane* category.

We began to talk and during the course of our very brief conversation, I became acutely aware of why he agreed to meet me. I suppose because I was the nerd who told him I loved him, he delusively thought he had the upper hand. In his erroneous presumption of me, he thought I'd be more than willing to *become popular*. It was the best he could do, or anyone can do to make a conjecture about someone with whom you do not routinely converse. As a result, little did he know, though I was an introvert and a nerd, I refused to allow my virtues to fall by the wayside all in the name of popularity.

Guilty as Charged

As an adult, I realized I was guilty of the very same thing. I *presumed* to know Christ. In fact, I felt confident that I knew Him.

There is only one word in this Scripture that gives it its depth. It is the very word that gives sustenance to eternal life. This word is *know*. How could I have reasonably claimed to know God? It is only in possessing a certainty, living an experience or acquiring a familiarity with someone or something that one can justifiably claim to *know* a person or a situation.

Communication is and should be the pivotal foundation upon which all relationships build and grow. In order to know anyone, communication is a must. No one can rightfully substantiate *I know him* as a result of only forced, infrequent or no communication. A desired communication that occurs regularly and over a long period of time fosters a relationship, and it is only in a relationship that one can truly assert to really know someone.

My default response to anyone who's ever asked me why I chose to be saved was always, *To get to heaven*. How pathetic is that answer? And at that, if the "knowing" part is what precedes eternal life, how in the world could I rationally respond with, *To get to heaven*. But that's exactly my point. In not acquiring familiarity with the Word of God and instituting a relationship with Jesus, I *voluntarily* rejected living the experience of knowing Him personally, thereby never quite possessing the certainty of eternal life.

It is true that ultimately, once all the days ordained for us have been expelled and we have fulfilled the propensity which God has instilled in each of us, heaven is our long-anticipated eternal glory. When I answered, *To get to heaven,* it was always my rescue answer. The catchall phrase that saved me. Those four words stifled any further deliberation about salvation in general which then worked in my favor as I simply did not possess the knowledge of proof via Scripture to sufficiently explain any question asked me regarding the Word of God. I did not *know* Christ that I may have given any other answer to that question.

But if someone were to ask me why I married the man I did, I wouldn't answer, *To have children*, even if that too were ultimately an end goal. In answering that question, I could easily give reasons like: "He's comical. He's considerate. He's a great provider. He's affectionate. He's faithful. He's a committed and loving dad." My answers actually substantiate that I *know* him well enough to provide a multitude of reasons as to why I married him.

I was unable to do the same with Jesus. Sure, I could have offered up generic answers such as He first loved me (See 1 John 4:19), He washed me whiter than snow (See Psalm 51:7), He died for my sins (See 1 Corinthians 15:3), and He rose from the dead (See Acts 10:40.) I could rattle off generic answers with the best of them—routine excerpts that I'd heard repeatedly in traditional Christmas songs, sermons I'd listened to over the years and Bible verses I'd helped my children memorize while in school. But that was all I could do—rattle off generic answers. They carried no personal meaning for me and I most certainly could not provide an explanation as to the meaning of the above Scripture. They were not applicable to my life. Those generic answers undoubtedly proved that I had no relationship with Christ Jesus.

Have we ever given thought to how much time we spend conversing with our dogs? We speak to them continuously. We ask them if they have to go potty, if they're hungry, if they are ready to go bye-bye or on a walk. We show them much affection by stroking them and telling them how much we love them and they actually respond with their tails what they feel in their hearts.

But yet, how much time do we devote to speaking with our Savior? Do we intentionally slip away to a quiet spot and shut ourselves off to the world and all the distractions of daily life in order to communicate with Him? When we routinely come before Him and actually communicate

Exercise

with Him, we find we can talk about anything. And for some, eventually, the forced, drag-your-feet meeting gives way to a yearning, can't-get-there-fast-enough desire to slip away. We no longer need to pencil in *a meeting with God at 5 p.m.* in our daily calendar. Loving communion with our Heavenly Father is what maintains the unwavering, daily return. And even during the course of the day, we find ourselves communicating with Him.

As a result, God becomes personal to us. When that happens, those generic answers that we once rattled off now touch the depth of our soul. We are actually feeling all that He sacrificed. His Word finally becomes applicable to our lives as we make it our aim to return our love faithfully and endlessly, the same as He does for us.

With the greeting of each new day, I am ever more confident in saying that I *know* Jesus Christ. I now know traits that define who God is. For example, God does not *choose* to love us—He *is* love (See 1 John 4:8.) He could no more *choose* to love someone than we could choose the DNA that comprises our very being. This is not to say that even if God were not love, He would not choose to love those He has given the very breath of life and who are made in His image. Furthermore, He is the God who avenges me (See Psalm 18:47.) I know that when I am faithless, He will remain faithful (See 2 Timothy 2:13.)

We must possess the yearning to expand any relationship. Our desire to know the person is what persuades us to seek it out. In our committed pursuit of that relationship, we are gifted the revelation of the beauty of the one with whom we are ever becoming better acquainted—an acquaintance that blossoms into a friendship that will endure a lifetime.

I am no longer required to render generic answers when speaking of Him. Only as a result of this personal relationship, bound by communication, am I equipped to provide answers that speak to His character and how His love for me actually affects me. These answers have a very personal meaning for me now, as they should for all Christians.

Exercise Setting an Example

But set an example for the believers in speech, in life, in love, in faith and in purity. – 1 Timothy 4:12

Identifying the Sin

In our premeditated effort to set an example, we understand that our example is something done outwardly and intentionally for all to see. I struggled to fulfill the expectation of "setting an example." The source of my struggle was my spiritual inability to grasp that change had to happen inwardly first for the example to be worthy of being seen outwardly.

Speech, life, love, faith and purity happen simultaneously when setting a godly example. I wrestled with this precept simply because nothing about my life was godly. These multiple failed attempts were because I had not identified the specific sin in my life that was causing a most undesirable example.

All Christians must recognize that the first step in the direction towards salvation is the admission that we are sinners. Secondly, we must acknowledge that without the death *and* resurrection of Jesus Christ we are still in our sins (See 1 Corinthians 15:17.) He is the grace that removes our sin. Asking to be forgiven is not a one-and-done process. As human beings, we are innate sinners. And we certainly sin an infinite number of times. It is then only reasonable to conclude that we must seek forgiveness on a regular basis.

I understood that in order to approach the throne of God, I needed to ask to be forgiven. In this request, though, I never confessed the *content* of the wrong I perpetrated. I didn't even know that the wrong I was committing was actually termed sin (See James 4:17.) I just asked to be forgiven. My prayer went something like, "Lord, I had another bad day today. I ask for Your forgiveness and help in not becoming a repeat offender." I always made certain that I sought forgiveness, and sometimes I immediately asked to be forgiven for my shortcomings. But inescapably, I'd commit the very same infraction within days or even hours. Obviously, there was no abiding change. For the life of me, I could not comprehend *why* I had become a repeat offender by committing the same wrong over and over again.

At times, I knew what was right, but I intentionally chose to do wrong. I didn't slip up. I meant to do it. But in doing it, I never knew it to be *sin* at the time. I just knew it was wrong and this was why I asked to be forgiven. Nor did I ever intend to offend the Lord. It was not my intent to take for granted the forgiveness I had been granted for the infractions I committed. My mind was void of any spiritual thought process. I just responded and reacted without giving any prior thought, unless intentional, to my conduct and my words.

I was angry but not at the Lord. I was angry because I'd been diligently seeking transformation in my life, yet it wasn't happening. Change is the totality of the renovation of our soul, and I did grasp that the change I so earnestly desired required the power of God through prayer.

I had no unreasonable expectation as to when this much-needed change would become a permanent part of my character. I reasoned that the amount of time this

Exercise

change necessitated, before I was routinely living it, could potentially equal the amount of time I had lived without the presence of God's precepts in my life. That was quite a long time.

In my anger and frustration, I began to self-reflect—something I had never devotedly taken the time to do. I began to really hone in on my offenses by actually reliving in my mind specific scenarios for which I had sought forgiveness. In so doing, I recognized a pattern. Clearly, I knew what my misdeeds were, but I had never before deliberately examined what might have generated my offense or whether my offenses had a tendency to occur in the same environment or even around the same people.

In reliving the scenarios, I relived the words, my reactions, the entirety of my wrong. The Holy Spirit revealed to me that in seeking God for forgiveness it is not enough to merely ask to be forgiven, but that I needed to tell God *how* I had sinned. Without doing that, I had failed to accept full responsibility for my actions. I was prone to place blame on others for my own shortcomings. Secondly, I needed to communicate what my actual offense was instead of asking God to forgive me as a *general* request.

In speaking the actual offense to God, I actually identified the *how*. I knew *what* my infraction was and even *where* it took place, but I had never examined *how* it was *sin* to

God. In answering the *how*—successful only by researching Scripture, I was able to pinpoint exactly the *sin* that grieved the Holy Spirit. And in knowing the how, I then knew precisely what to pray so that an enduring change might come forth.

Because of this revelation, my prayers began to sound like: "I snapped at him. I didn't speak out of love but out of retaliation. Help me to speak words that encourage, not discourage . . . words that uplift, not debase . . . words that give life, not death."

Change is a long-awaited, overdue, much-needed, unpleasant process—and a lengthy one at that. Change necessitates that we start and restart an undetermined number of times. In the process of starting and restarting, we gain wisdom, we gain tenacity, we gain godly character. We no longer concentrate on our present flaws, but rather we concentrate on the lifelong promises of a life lived in a godly manner.

Remain in the Maintain Status

All of us long to change ourselves in one way or another whether we admit it or not. This truth is proven time and time again by the enormous number of people who participate in the worldwide, ever-popular New Year's Resolution. We make commitments that, at times, consume

Exercise

and dominate our lives. We partake along with family and friends in resolutions to lose weight, stop smoking or develop shipshape organizational skills.

We start with good intentions by strictly adhering to our plan for change. We set goals that are realistically attainable, and we begin our endeavor with much vigor. Finally, after much sacrifice, devotion and time, we meet our objective—but then comes the *hard* part, *maintaining* that change. Yes, that's right. The easy part is done—achieving the goal. Now begins the arduous task of *maintaining* that which was changed. The accomplished goal leaves us feeling like a new person. Sadly, however, all too often this feeling is short-lived.

Recently, I lost a considerable amount of weight. Periodically, I wear a pair of shorts that fit me at my heaviest. Thankfully, they are equipped with a drawstring as elastic would be problematic in keeping them around my waist as opposed to around my ankles. In the privacy of my own home, I don't merely try them on, I actually wear them.

The first time my husband witnessed me wearing these overly huge shorts, his first reaction was laughter. He then told me how ridiculous I looked and inquired why I would ever feel the need to wear them. I explained to him that though pictures speak a thousand words, they have this great inability to aid us in actually *reliving* the flood of *emotions* we experienced at the time the picture was taken. In physically wearing these shorts, I am reminded of the potential health problems inherent in carrying the additional weight. Also, as I pull the shorts out from my waist, expanding them to the furthest point possible, I can suddenly "feel" the weight I managed to gain which then leads me to the realization that if I had not begun a weight loss program when I did, the chances of never having begun are great. The shorts suddenly elicit old emotions that make me feel embarrassed, unhealthy, lazy and weak as I lugged around all that weight. Oddly enough, those emotions encourage me not to revert to my old self—physically or emotionally. They serve to remind me of the laborious struggle, persistent fortitude, and burdensome sacrifices I made to achieve the goal. These very same efforts are crucial to *maintain* the change.

Maintaining change actually becomes far more difficult than the effort exhausted in reaching the goal because we don't comprehend that the once short-lived sacrifice made to reach the goal is the same *lifelong* sacrifice needed to *maintain* the change. We must utilize the same staying power we became all too familiar with in achieving our objective.

A goal is short-term. Maintaining is lifelong. In order to remain in a "maintain" status, the desired change must become a condition of the heart. For it to become a condition of the heart, it has to become a conscious way of life.

At the onset of the goal we are working towards, we live emotions like discouragement, hopelessness and downheartedness. This is primarily because, early on, we are not able to physically see the results of our efforts. In our struggle to initialize the goal, we may understandably start and restart an undetermined number of times. But once we do finally reach our goal, it would seem logical that we maintain the change, lifelong, because we have amazingly become masterfully proficient in the measures taken to attain the short-term goal. We have become adept in recognizing and defeating the temptations that long to derail us. In the same way, instituting the necessary means that enable us to live the godly life for which we yearn begets the example worthy to be seen and followed by all. Our example serves as a witness that we are choosing to *maintain* the change that we so valiantly fought to possess.

Doing the Right Thing?

Scenario 1

Harold was being bullied by Jack. On this particular day, Tom, an upper classman, witnessed what he initially thought was joking amongst friends. Suddenly, to Tom's surprise, Jack pushed Harold up against a locker. Tom rushed to the locker where the boys stood and told Jack to back off. Jack then squared off with Tom, who then grabbed Jack by the shirt. Jack pushed back, and a fight ensued.

Scenario 2

Barbara didn't watch Priscilla's children on a recurring basis. However, the last time Barbara had watched them, Priscilla noticed Barbara smoking, as she made her way to the front door. Priscilla confronted Barbara, reminding her that she had asked her not to smoke while the children were in her care. Priscilla explained that while she knew Barbara smoked, she trusted that Barbara would honor her request.

Barbara scornfully replied that she had given thought to Priscilla's request and decided she would never allow someone to dictate what she could and could not do in her own home.

Priscilla retaliated with unspeakable words and ended the conversation by telling Barbara that if she couldn't understand that the request was solely about the health of her children and not some type of controlling request, Barbara would never watch her children again.

Scenario 3

The subdivision rule mandated that when walking a dog, the owner must leash the dog and pick up the dog's waste.

Exercise

George walked his dog daily and knowingly disregarded both of the established rules.

Aaron was washing his car when he noticed George walking away after his dog had just done his business in Aaron's yard. Aaron quickly assessed the situation and noticing the absence of doggie bags concluded George must've forgotten them. He ran to the garage, grabbed a grocery bag and kindly began cleaning up the waste. George continued his leisurely walk.

Aaron called out to George who turned and began his return toward Aaron. Aaron kindly said to George he had already picked up his dog's waste as a favor to George when he noticed he didn't have bags with him. George laughed. And Aaron, offended by his laughter, became hostile with George. As George began to walk away once again, Aaron yelled promising threats.

Summary

The protagonist in each scenario made choices for scrupulous reasons. Tom courageously defended an innocent person. Priscilla sought to protect her children from an unhealthy environment. Aaron upheld the subdivision deed restrictions. But despite that, each one ultimately unleashed a reprehensible example.

Doing the right thing isn't always equivalent to setting a good example.

Tom resorted to physical measures to thwart bullying. Priscilla spoke unmentionable words in front of her children in her effort to protect them, and Aaron became hostile toward a neighbor because of the neighbor's neglect for common courtesy.

Delivering a hurried retort allows for no prior thought to the consequences of our actions and words. In the heat of the moment, it seems an unreasonable expectation to stop long enough to contemplate alternative responses in sticky situations. Though there are situations that in the time demanded to plan a response, danger could result; most times we have the opportunity to think before we act or speak.

We sometimes respond unnecessarily because we refuse to permit someone else to have the last word or the upper hand. We deceivingly believe that in granting our offender such power that we are weak, but this warped emotion is rooted in pride. God does not bless pride—only humility.

As we begin to ingest the Holy Word and converse with our Heavenly Father, we invisibly weave the precepts of God into our very being. The precepts lived are the endeavor filled: "Be holy, because I am holy" (1 Peter 1:16). Our lives will slowly, but surely, reveal the emulation of Christ

Exercise

Jesus as we become deliberate in seeking the Holy Spirit's daily guidance. As we yield to His guidance, we promote the power to know if a response is ever truly needed, and our obedience will be sure to unveil a godly example worthy to be seen and followed by all.

As we maintain purity because of our obedience to God's Holy Word, our faith only multiplies as we become the recipient of His promises. As long as our lives glorify God, we produce with a conscious effort, a worthy example. Our speech, life, love, faith and purity always happen together and always happen simultaneously. It is only in our outward example of speech, life and love that our inward faith and purity are exhibited.

CHAPTER THREE

Not

Bring honor Not shame to His name.

The Company We Keep

*Do **not** be misled: "Bad company corrupts good character."*
– 1 Corinthians 15:33 (author emphasis)

Of course we love the company of others. But do we stop to consider this particular verse as we share our time with them? If we do, how do *we* define bad? Do we conveniently define bad as something that does not include the specific company we've chosen to keep in an effort to justify our continued relationship with them?

In bringing no shame to His name, we must consider what this requires of us that we might be victorious in this end goal. We must heed the forewarning that we will *inevitably* be corrupted by bad company, and we must have a unified understanding of *bad* as anything that is opposite the Word of God thus pulling an individual away from a godly life. If we maintain this understanding, we are certain to bring no shame to His name.

It is of utmost importance to reiterate the understanding of "bad"—opposite the Word of God. This concept of bad is relevant to those *Christians* whose goal it is to submit to the guidance of the Holy Spirit. It is the influence of the bad practice that makes bad company. We only benefit from the Holy Spirit's guidance to abandon the company whose practice serves to corrupt the character of the individual.

In bringing no shame to His name, we must first be sure that our own name has no affiliation with shame because as soon as it does, our name too brings shame to Him. Just as Christ is known by His name inasmuch as His name encompasses all that He is, our name not only serves the same purpose for us but additionally and undoubtedly encompasses all that Christ is—or in some cases, all that He is not in our lives.

We must consider whether we are able to scrupulously self-reflect to ensure that *our* name has no affiliation with shame. Our self-reflection should not be based on the *opinions* we have of ourselves because obviously these opinions are biased and we can easily justify them. We must, without rose-colored glasses, scrutinize our featured character, our practiced values, and our uninhibited tolerance. If we are purely objective when considering these exercised traits then the interpretation of ourselves will be factually accurate.

When someone hears our name, instantaneously, a deduction is made about us. How do others accurately arrive at a conclusion regarding who we are? The more obvious answers might include the tone we use in response to others and the words that accompany the tone, the choices we make, the love we have for others and last, but certainly not least, the company we keep. If we are ever mindful to conduct ourselves in a manner worthy of the gospel of Christ (See Philippians 1:27) then the concluding deduction others make about us will undoubtedly be true and unerring.

Deductions about us are made by people who know us well, but can also be made by those who barely know us or who do not know us at all. Regardless of *who* draws the conclusion, the responsibility is ours to help ensure that all deductions made about us undeniably reflect what is in our heart. If we are choosing to fill our mind and heart with the things of God, we clinch the goal in bringing no shame to our name or His.

My husband and I very much enjoy playing cards, though my husband will attest to the fact that even after all these years, I still play cards like a novice. Nonetheless, many years ago, we frequently played cards with one couple in particular. This couple liked to drink. I'm not a drinker, nor have I ever been. I've simply never had any interest in it. However, oddly enough, I began to drink—but only in the company of this particular couple. I was never pressured into drinking, nor did I ever feel that if I didn't participate in drinking, I wouldn't be accepted.

In looking back on that part of my life, I cannot recall any apparent reason why I began to consume alcohol. I suppose I could blame curiosity, but why after all these years would I suddenly become curious? Even in my teenage years when my peers frequently engaged in alcohol consumption, I never did. If curiosity were my motive, it makes more sense that my curiosity would have spiked when I was a teenager leading me to join them. Yet, as a teenager, I chose not to participate in drinking.

I realize now and am confident in my conclusion that the enemy always has a plan. He fights tooth and nail and never surrenders his goal to kill, to steal and to destroy. He feverishly works overtime to strike those who are drawing nearer to our Lord and Savior. As an adult, I was sneakily lured into the temptation of drinking and though a choice I didn't regret then, I certainly do now.

Because we moved away, we no longer affiliated ourselves with that couple and I stopped drinking—all because we no longer kept their company. I was living proof of just one of God's most absolute truths. As much as we tell ourselves as practicing Christians that we will never partake in the bad practices of the company we keep or even that we're strong enough to combat whatever bad things we're exposed to, we end up doing the very thing we said we'd never do. Under no circumstances are we exempt from being corrupted regardless of the vows we make to never become a participant in the thing's others choose to practice.

This isn't to say that there won't be situations during the course of our lives, perhaps even within our own families, where we must be in the presence of bad company. It is to say, however, that *repeatedly choosing* to be in the presence of bad company inevitably corrupts good character. We should, without fail, heed all God's commands and all His forewarnings. Living in His will keeps us from sin and a great deal of regret.

Are *We* the Cause?

We, as Christians, could very well be the bad company that others find themselves in the presence of, though we refuse to discredit *ourselves* as such. Most ordinarily we mistakenly perceive bad company solely as the visible wrongs that bad company practice. But, irrefutably, being in bad company includes all that we hear as well.

My youngest daughter was recently hired at a well-known department store. Only three weeks into her job and only her second time working the register, she innocently became the target of a humiliating situation.

Apparently, the customer in her line had been told by a floor associate that the item she was purchasing was on sale. When the register did not recognize it as a sale item, the customer attempted to use a store coupon. The coupon also failed to apply a discount, though my daughter made numerous attempts to validate it.

Because my daughter was new, she explained to the customer that she'd like to solicit the help of a seasoned employee to ensure that she herself was not doing something incorrectly in processing the coupon. The seasoned employee explained that the coupon could not be used in conjunction with that particular name brand item. The customer, unexpectedly, became obnoxiously loud and irate—so loud that she drew the attention of customers at the other end of the store even though she was with what appeared to be her four young children. My daughter stood there helpless, along with the customer's children, as she anticipated the customer's anger would be short-lived as she continued with the checkout, but she was wrong. The customer continued her disgruntled rant with unspeakable words until she exited the store.

Not

My Christian daughter's first thought as she attempted to digest and process what she just witnessed was that there was no way that customer was a Christian. Her justifiable conclusion was based on the customer's ungodly reaction.

Though this incident is *not* how we most often define bad company, we need to conceptualize that bad company includes all we hear as well as all we see. However, in an effort to not discredit ourselves as such, we deceptively tell ourselves that our words in no way qualify as bad company. Not only do they qualify, they are just as influentially bad.

I know this because all too often *I* was the bad company that my children were around. Though a Christian, I often responded in the very same manner as that customer. And though never publicly—as if somehow that lessens the severity of the wrong—I spoke such words, as did the customer, to my very own husband in the presence of my very own children. The people I love the most in my life, I subjected the most to my bad company. And disgracefully, I brought unspeakable shame to His name, the One in whose image I was made.

Had I continued in my ungodly attitude, the bad company I proved to be was bound to have corrupted the character of my children, thus perpetuating the shame brought to His name. We must grasp the absolute certainty that the witness we bear—all too soon—can potentially become the life our children lead.

Be Not Offended

*My conscience is clear, but that does **not** make me innocent.*
– 1 Corinthians 4:4 (author emphasis)

As we strive daily to bring no shame to His name, it is vital that we maintain a clear conscience. To successfully do so is effortless when we ourselves define the standards that preserve our clear conscience. Periodically, we permit even ourselves to roam outside our own defined parameters.

At first, guilt emerges when we overstep these boundaries. But as we give in to our self-encouraged and recurrent thoughts, our guilt subsides. Our conscience is made clear again as we pledge, ineffectually, to uphold it exclusively as thought.

One very lofty and indisputable character attribute of our Savior is that He knows all, even our thoughts (See Psalm 94:11.) Despite this, we convince ourselves that because no one can *visualize* the sinful and evil *thoughts* we entertain, we're blameless. However, though our thoughts cannot be seen, eventually they are evidenced in what we do or what we say.

When loved ones share the error of our ways, we often become offended and angry. However, the withholding of this now shared information can potentially lead to an irreparable harm in our relationships. This harm defined: we

Not

illogically conclude sometimes that if in our own perception our conscience is clear then our choices must apparently be good and right. Our indignant response to the loved one's honesty shuts us down as well as them.

My husband and I lived a very preventable but potentially irreparable situation in our marriage due to his unknown understanding of what constitutes a guiltless conscience. Only God's Word enlightens us concerning the mandates that will forever accomplish a pure conscience.

"You're not good enough. You never will be," I heard her say. My husband and I heard the very same statement as we stood together in the very same room—and suddenly the room loudly silenced after the abusive attack on me. The drive home was mostly silent aside from me explaining to him that his silence after the attack could be interpreted only one way—that he felt the same way she did. I told him if he agreed with that comment that remaining in any relationship out of pure obligation always results in misery, and that we certainly should not subject our children to such an environment.

The next few weeks, our home was filled with silence broken only by periodic arguing. Ironically enough, our arguments never centered on the assassinating words the woman had abusively spoken about me. When we did peacefully speak to one another, the pain I thought I managed to bury suddenly resurfaced and the once peaceful conversation turned into, yet again, hateful arguing. The pain erupted frequently because I felt rejected and unworthy by his failure to defend the one he had taken in marriage.

The cyclical arguing and silence that continued was fueled by me. After some time, I realized my husband was not going to be the one to initiate the much-needed discussion regarding my rollercoaster ride of emotions. So with reluctant intent, I approached him—this time without tears as my heart toward him had hardened. The pain that had visited and revisited me since the woman attacked me had turned completely into anger. I explained to him that after the attack, I equated his silence to him not loving me.

His response was defensive rather than compassionate and empathetic. His defensiveness ignited because a loved one had pointed out the error of his ways, and his once guiltless conscience suddenly became guilty. He was offended. In his eagerness, he failingly tried to defend himself. He attempted to justify his non-responsiveness to this woman's insult by saying things like: *Consider the source, her opinion doesn't matter,* and *she has no bearing on our relationship.*

As he continued to rant in his *own* defense, I wondered where this defense was on my behalf weeks ago. I was thinking to myself he could fight to defend *himself,* but that he had chosen not to fight to defend me, his wife. At that time, the only rational conclusion I could surmise was that he thought more of himself than he did his own wife.

I don't know that I'll ever understand why he remained silent during that incident, but I do know that I carried much anger, bitterness and malice towards him for many, many years—which resulted in the tables being turned. I, too, had been wrongly living with a clear conscience; one that was defined by my own standards.

It wasn't necessarily the *feelings* of anger, bitterness and malice that forced a guilty conscience in the eyes of God but rather *harboring* those feelings, especially for such an extended period of time. Instead, we must heed Ephesians 4:26, "Do not let the sun go down while you are still angry."

In the lifetime process of renovating our souls, if we drench ourselves in God's Word and live obediently to Him from the beginning, we spare ourselves an abundance of sin as well as an abundance of heartache. His principles unfailingly lead us in preserving our clear conscience. In order that we bring no shame to His name, we must maintain this pure conscience.

Our Anger Can Lead to Regrettable Expression

*In your anger, do **not** sin.* – Psalm 4:4 (author emphasis)

Anger. We've all been there, even the best of us. But how adept are we at not sinning in our anger? Though anger should not be one of our most common responses, it is, in fact, an emotion that is a very normal response. I love this Scripture simply because it is the very confirmation that *everyone* expresses anger.

In fact, the very words *in your anger* are representative of the anticipation that anger *will*, at some point, manifest itself in our lives—for some, more than others. Anger is undeniably a chosen response, though at times we would beg to differ. We would argue instead that in certain situations anger is downright unpreventable—a response that is so very sudden it seems we are incapable of contemplating an alternative reaction. Therefore, we assure ourselves that anger happens without warning.

If we can concede that there are any number of ways in which to respond to all the situations that life presents, then logically, we should be able to concede that anger is a voluntary response. Most times, the cause of our anger is the failed attempt of others to meet the expectations *we* have placed on *them.*

Expectations are an essential part of life. They serve to set boundaries and limitations to keep others from harm and regret and to teach them responsibility. We set expectations for others and likewise expectations are set for us.

I place expectations on my children every day. In our home, our children are not rewarded for meeting our expectations. This concept also holds true in everyday life. We simply do what is expected of us without reward. For example, we are expected to tell the truth, practice fidelity in marriage, and pay our bills. It's how we function and thrive. My children know that expectations are not optional, hence *expect*ations. They understand such expectations as homework must be completed, bedrooms picked up, and bathroom towels hung. When they fail to meet these expectations, I have a choice in how I respond.

As Christians, we must be cognizant of how we respond to unmet expectations. The Word of God is very specific in the expectation *not* to sin in our anger. But far too often for many people, anger and sin coincide as people disobey God's Word by sinning in expressing their anger.

If we are really honest with ourselves, the complications that anger us most often are not life altering. In fact, they are usually quite petty and insignificant in the broad scope of life and so anger seems a rather harsh choice. So most times, it is a response that is simply not justifiable.

In the event that we deem anger as the only justifiable response or when our impulsive anger forces our inability to search for a less brutal response, we must, at the very least, be mindful not to sin. The point at which anger generates unforgiveness, retaliation, regrettable expression, abuse, addiction or hatred is the point when we have voluntarily committed sin in our anger. We need not only repent, but also turn from the wicked practices that our anger induces. We must force ourselves to simply walk away *before* responding to any situation that could potentially ignite our anger.

Our goal should be to make every concentrated effort to confront and rectify a situation before it ever leads to anger. Though anger is a very normal response, it should not be a frequently chosen response. Justified or not, in our anger, let us not sin.

We Benefit From Non-violated Boundaries

*When he gave the sea its boundary so the waters would **not** overstep his command.* – Proverbs 8:29 (author emphasis)

Boundaries include the abstract life limits that assist us in making those final choices that steer us from adversity, but most times we think of boundaries as established physical dividing lines that serve as borders. Most homes occupy land with buried pins that identify where property lines begin and end. As we travel the highways and byways, the yellow and white lines, some dotted, some solid, render themselves as borders that remind us to maintain our present lane without carelessly weaving to and fro. We are inundated with boundaries, though we often don't

Not

recognize them as such because they are an inseparable part of our lives.

Most boundaries, physical or abstract are implemented by those in authority. And God in His authority has set forth boundaries. In establishing these boundaries, His unadulterated intention is to support us in living obediently thus keeping us from harm. He fully understands that life is difficult at best. Countless situations unfold in life over which we have no control. But in those that we can control, our choice to heed the boundaries God has decreed in love will keep us from harm as we live obediently before our Father.

As children, our choices were restricted solely by our parents' rules—rules that required us to live within certain confines as defined by our parents. At times, we simply despised these boundaries as we felt they only served to interfere in all that we longed to do. However, when we chose to break the rules or go outside the boundaries, we voluntarily subjected ourselves to unavoidable consequences. With love and pure intention, our parents set forth these rules and boundaries to spare us from these consequences.

Once we have children of our own, we suddenly grasp the need to instill boundaries regardless of the age and stage our children are growing into and through. We are now choosing to impose the very same rules our parents once did, on our own children to shield them from harm. Our Heavenly Father has implemented life boundaries for the very same reason; He longs to spare His beloved children regret, pain and heartbreak.

The entirety of God's Word is a boundary—a guide to obedience—and the limit set forth is a safeguard. Some of the harm from which He longs to keep us is apparent. Some are not. We overstep His command when we neglect His boundaries. In doing so, we elect disobedience thereby exposing ourselves to potential harm. Nothing good stems from disobedience. In choosing to forgo God's boundaries, we do so with the certitude that a consequence will result. A consequence lived; we wish we would have chosen to avoid.

Though God's Word includes such an abundance of guidance, we still manage to convince ourselves that what was applicable in biblical times is not relevant in today's society. Rest assured that the only thing that has changed from biblical times to now is the century. We can know with absolute certainty that for every circumstance in life, God has already instituted a boundary. A non-violated boundary accommodates a two-fold purpose: to keep us from harm while maintaining our obedience.

Salvation in no way exempts us from God's boundaries. If a practicing Christian were somehow exempt from these boundaries, it only stands to reason that he voluntarily sets himself up for the possibility of unnecessary pain and regret. Life, in and of itself, is difficult. And for those who are Christians, wisdom is offered in the form of guidance. Salvation necessitates that we heed these life limits as established by God's boundaries in every effort to live a most fulfilled life.

His Spiritual Sufficiency

***Not** that we are sufficient of ourselves to think of anything as being from ourselves, but our sufficiency is from God.* – 2 Corinthians 3:5, KJV (author emphasis)

It is always of utmost importance to recognize the verb tense of each and every Scripture contained in the Word of God. The verb tense is the enlightenment of the promises that we have *already* received, we will *eventually* receive, or we are and will continue to be *in the midst* of receiving. The beauty of 2 Corinthians 3:5 is the illumination that we are and will forever be receiving His sufficiency.

We might be inclined to understand the word *sufficiency* solely in its physical connotation. We think of sufficiency as the means by which life is sustained. For example, wild animals, ocean life and the birds of the air are responsible for acquiring their own sustenance. If their food chain *sufficiency* is depleted, these creatures then die.

Our hope for our children is to one day become accountable in securing their own sufficiency, but in their formative years, we as parents are our children's physical sufficiency. A considerable part of our parental role is providing our children with the food that nourishes them, the clothing that covers them, the shelter that protects them, the schooling that educates them, and the love that promotes their well-being and security.

But in order that *we* may provide and supply, we ourselves must receive the necessary sufficiency. God is this very sufficiency. He is the *primary* source of all provision that sustains our lives. We are merely the *secondary* source of our children's provision.

Those of us who are actively seeking God in all aspects of our lives and who long to remain within the parameters of obedience, as part of the renovation of our soul, invite God to lovingly ordain all aspects of our lives. The long-awaited events and circumstances that unfold during the course of our lives are nothing of ourselves. That long-sought-after job is awarded by the hand of God. The loan we desperately need is approved because of His favor. Our emotional, physical and spiritual healing is granted because of His mercy. In seeking God, we are purposely seeking His guidance and accepting His will above our own, for our lives, as He sees best.

Sometimes, we forget to acknowledge God as our sustenance. Sometimes, we innocently take for granted all that He, alone, bestows upon us. But all that we see and touch during the course of our day is traceable to the hand of God. The running water to shower, the pantry filled with food, and the bed we rest upon serve to remind us daily that God is our physical sufficiency.

And if He is our physical sufficiency, *how much more* is He our spiritual sufficiency? We are not comparing the quantities of each sufficiency. Rather, we are acknowledging that His gift of salvation is the single most paramount spiritual sufficiency given.

Our salvation is not an afterthought. As a matter of fact, God does nothing as an afterthought. "I make known the end from the beginning, from ancient times, what is still to come" (Isaiah 46:10).

God knew from the beginning that Eve would convincingly partake of the fruit from the tree of knowledge of good and evil. As a result, He knew beforehand that His Son would serve as our spiritual sufficiency. He had to. The reconciliation needed is the purpose of salvation. God knew that He had to reconcile us to Him "…by Christ's physical body through death to present you holy in his sight, without blemish and free from accusation" (Colossians 1:22). The only way we are without blemish is to be without sin. And, "without the shedding of blood there is no forgiveness" (Hebrews 9:22). And we know that the forgiveness granted is for the sin committed. "This is my blood of the covenant, which is poured out for many for the forgiveness of sins" (Matthew 26:28). His Son had to die.

Christ alone is our spiritual sufficiency. A synonymous term for sufficiency is *adequate*. *The dictionary defines adequate as "able to satisfy a requirement" (Def. 1. Webster's II new Riverside university dictionary, The Riverside Publishing Company, 1984, p. 78).* Jesus Christ was the requirement (See 2 Corinthians 5:21.) His blood satisfied the need, once for all, to present us without blemish and free from accusation before God the Father.

Christ is the solitary derivation from which all our sufficiency flows. He is physical and spiritual healing. He is grace and mercy granted to an undeserving humanity. He causes our barns to be filled with every kind of provision. He is faith when we are faithless. He is strength when we are weak. He is our intercessor before God the Father.

Though we indirectly contribute the physical sufficiency to sustain life, God is the direct source of all physical and spiritual sufficiency. God graciously provides for us, and we in turn provide for ourselves and our loved ones. We are humbled in the realization that we are not sufficient of ourselves to think of *anything* as being from ourselves.

Not

Anything is all-inclusive. Anything is everything. Praise our Almighty God for His sufficiency that sustains us both physically and spiritually.

CHAPTER FOUR

One and Done

One and done.

I've often wondered just how many saved people misunderstand our salvation as a one-and-done devotion versus a lifestyle. The events of our lives lead us to Christ. He then graciously extends salvation to a truly penitent heart. Suddenly, we feel peace with the expectancy that our lives will be forever changed—and we live the one-and-done misconception that once saved, our part is done, and God is responsible for the rest. What we fail to understand is that our obligation to live a life that is a representation of our salvation has only just begun and will never end.

Nothing worth having is ever accomplished in a one-and-done mode. Our time and effort are the deposit made into the investment of anything worth having and anything worth having always yields a profit. But, in neglecting to deposit our time and effort, we are choosing a one-and-done mentality which in turn never yields a profit.

I have always considered the one-and-done mentality a lazy man's choice. I also think it simpleminded not to finish what is started. If something is important enough to initiate, then obviously the actual completion of it will serve only to benefit us. I recognize that in order to reap the long-term benefits of that which is meaningful to me, *I* am accountable for the necessary care and maintenance that will provide the desired longevity.

For example, I do not take for granted the work the Lord provides my husband or his health which enables him to work for our provision. When we make a purchase, regardless of the expense, it is most meaningful because I know that God is the sufficiency for that provision so I take care of what God provides. If we purchase a car, the oil is changed as directed by the manufacturer, the tires inflated with the necessary amount of air and the tune-ups performed at the prescribed mileage. My coffee maker is cleansed with vinegar every six months, and the furnace filter is replaced when the orange light indicator glows on my thermostat. Such maintenance, derived from maintain, is never one and done.

This same care and maintenance we take to extend the usage of those things that make our lives easier is also crucial to our relationships. Especially in marriage, our utmost attention is given to the necessary precautionary measures to ensure the longevity of our marriages. We are careful to remain faithful—both physically and mentally, we joyfully and regularly engage in communication, we practice compromise, we encourage one another, we are truthful and upfront and we strive to keep peace within our marriage.

I never included myself in the community of those who executed this one and done practice because I could easily prove otherwise. I avidly and routinely performed the necessary care and maintenance to sustain the longevity of anything God so graciously equipped my life with. To me, this was all the substantial proof required to exclude myself from the one and done community.

I did, however, experience an aha moment, a life-altering epiphany that pre-empted a most radical change. I realized that my refusal to practice one and done applied only to everyday things I could see, touch and interact with. I came to understand that the absence of all that I desperately needed spiritually had one and done stamped all over it. I most certainly *was* that person that maintained the one and done mentality in my *spiritual* life. I was saved and expected God to take care of the rest—whatever the rest may have been. It isn't that I was taught this way of thinking. Actually, I wasn't "taught" anything regarding my personal spiritual life. But I did come to realize that many of us live our spiritual life in that very same one-and-done mentality.

We find ourselves in some sort of predicament—one that can sometimes be most familiar to us as we repeatedly fall into the very same situation. Perhaps we find ourselves emotionally starved for love, affection or acceptance. Maybe we just need the favor of God to rest upon us. Whatever our need in that moment, it leads us longing for the help of Jesus. We concentrate on getting through just this one adversity or this one failure, and then all will be well—assuring ourselves this episode in our life will not become a rerun. But all too often, the one and done mentality practices an unwelcome pattern.

We begin to read God's Word in search of answers that apply to our current need. We seek the face of God, yearning for His guidance. A part of this guidance is the revelation by the Holy Spirit that we have not been mindful of the choices we make. We realize that our unwise choices are the reason we are at His feet. And these poor choices are the reason we repeatedly fall into these same predicaments.

A length of time passes and our situation improves. We attribute the resolution to God's power and grace. Thereafter we conveniently slip away from the very short-lived and temporary commitment to Him. A length of time passes and we once again find ourselves in another predicament—maybe even the one we know all too well, or maybe even a new one. We fall before Him, crying out to Him for His presence in our lives. Once again, we begin to read and study and reenter into a minimal relationship with Jesus. This minimal commitment to Jesus is fleeting and trifling. Did it ever occur to us that as we fervently pursue resolution through reading, studying and seeking God, we are actually living in obedience? Sin can be the origin of many problems, and obedience steers us away from sin—always. But once things begin to look up for us, we depart from the transitory godly lifestyle.

We commit so much more easily to anything and everything temporal. For example, we get sick and see a doctor. He diagnoses our malady and prescribes an antibiotic. He states that after only a few days of taking them, we will definitely notice a dramatic improvement in how we feel. But he explicitly forewarns that in order to *effectively* treat the malady and to *remain* in a state of wellness, we must finish the entire course of antibiotics. So, under his advisement, we finish the entire prescription and our good health returns.

We are *faithful to obey* the physician's instructions. Do we not concede then that the way in which we treat our earthly maladies may just parallel the way in which our spiritual maladies *should* be treated? We seek a physician in both, each one in turn provides counsel, and in our *obedience*, we anticipate a remedy. The major and most impactful dissimilarity is that the earthly antibiotics necessitate a specified amount of time, but the remedy our Heavenly Physician prescribes requires a lifetime that we remain in a state of wellness.

Is it that we come and go in our spiritual dedication because the obedience—the reading and the studying become too much for us in the way of time devoted to the practice? Is it that we can always justify a more productive way to spend our time? Is it that in that short time devoted to His word and prayer, we've suddenly mastered how to live? Is it that, secretly, the obedience is something that actually interferes with the choices we *wish* to make?

If we've answered yes to any one of those questions, did we at the very least gain the understanding that while taking in the Word and seeking Him, we ultimately made better choices during that short amount of time? Can we acknowledge that life did get better in choosing to abide by His precepts? Are we able to set aside our prized arrogance long enough to admit that we have not, in fact, really mastered how to live?

Everyone is all too familiar with the one-and-done concept. We purchase a gym membership, only to attend one workout session. We commit to diet and give up one week later. After only one date, we foolishly surmise he cannot be the one for me. We choose not to commit for any number of reasons that we think are logically justifiable. Those reasons likely include the time or tenacity required or our own fierce pride and pomposity. Of course, such traits never prove fruitful. We simply cannot live a spiritual *life* in a one-and-done mindset. In choosing this route, life is not manageable, fulfilling and joyful. It's a given that life isn't easy. We need all the help we can get. And who better to give us that promising help and guidance than Jesus Christ our Lord?

God's Instruction Manual

I will never forget your precepts, for by them you have preserved my life. – Psalm 119:93

My husband and I purchased a small entryway bench for our utility room. The size of the bench is what initially attracted me to it. In my thinking, the small size would lend itself to effortless assembly thus requiring very little of my husband's time. I assumed these two very enticing reasons would work in my favor when requesting that he put it together for me. I could not have been more wrong. I was deceived by the size of the bench; I foolishly equated its size with the amount of labor needed to construct such a small piece of furniture. I have come to the conclusion that all assembly is never easy and always requires more time than originally planned.

My husband started by gathering all the tools catalogued in the directions. He unpacked the box and neatly separated the bolts and pieces of furniture as instructed. About fifteen to twenty minutes into the project, I heard him begin to grumble. I knew from past experience that the assembly was already frustrating him. I approached him to ask if there was anything I could do to help. He politely refused. As we begin to talk about how things are never easy, we exchange comments like:

I wish this were easier to assemble.
I wish the instructions were easier to understand.
Why does this have to take so long?
Why couldn't this have been already assembled when delivered?

Later that night while I was praying, I began to thank God for my husband. Thankful he has never been the kind of man to blamingly disclose his frustration because of the difficulty in completing a project. He doesn't swear, throw things or vent his frustration towards me.

As I continued praying, I began talking about how instruction manuals, in general, are so difficult to understand. I rambled on about not knowing if the difficulty lies with the person interpreting the instructions or with the author of the instruction manual itself. I decided I may never know the answer to that question. But I do know, as a result of the revelation given by the Holy Spirit, God's Word is also an instruction manual.

This was a wow moment for me. I had never thought of the Bible as an instruction manual. I suppose it's because my Bible wasn't packed with an abundance of packing peanuts and delivered neatly in a box with a piece of paper attached to the front which read *Instruction Manual*. But the more I contemplated it, the more it seemed to fit the criteria to be defined as such.

Why are instruction manuals included with items? They are included solely for the purpose of assembly. Without the manual, we just have separate parts and pieces, which in and of themselves, serve no function. A correctly deciphered instruction manual is required to achieve a fully assembled, functional item that serves the purpose for which it is intended.

Believers, in a constant state of assembly, should be striving to achieve the purpose *God* intended for our lives. As we are in desperate need of spiritual assembly, we reference God's instruction manual—His Holy Word. In doing so, we eventually fulfill the dedicated purpose of the manual; we become the spiritual being God so intended.

While still in prayer, the Holy Spirit also revealed to me that in our desire as goal-oriented Christians to live in alignment with the ordinances of God, we express our frustration in the very same statements such as: *I wish this were easier* or *why does this have to take so long*. We are baffled as to why obedience takes so long and is so difficult to incorporate into our daily lives. The answer is because we fight it. In wishing the instructions were easier to understand, sometimes we are actually hoping to formulate a way to still fulfill the desires of the flesh while living obediently. But in realizing that can never reasonably happen because carnal living is in direct opposition to spiritual living, we begin to understand we will never be easy to assemble. For others, the difficulty in assembly is our rejection to submit to obedience. Our parts and pieces cannot be separate from Him. God is the necessary component that our parts and pieces mandate to become spiritually fully functional.

The power of the Holy Spirit manufactures our spirituality. In this lifelong undertaking, we soon discover that the parts and pieces required for construction don't seem properly sized for our individual assembly. These seemingly irregular pieces are not to blame for the discomfort we are experiencing rather it is the stretching and growing of ourselves as necessitated by the manufacturer's specifications. Eventually, our parts and pieces will fit together most perfectly enabling us to serve the function God intended for each of us.

In seeking salvation, are we not ultimately seeking an instruction manual? We long to find someone who knows the wrongs we've committed and yet is willing to forgive us those wrongs, all the while loving us. The hope is that the instruction manual will help to mend us, putting the parts and pieces together, maybe even adding some new ones—anything that will allow us to feel whole.

So many of us arrive broken at the feet of Christ and fall before Him crying out for help. At some point in our lives, it has become apparent to us that we have not made the choices that allow us to live life fully and joyfully. With this revelation, our hope is to gain acceptance, peace, wholeness and joy while eliminating rejection, upheaval, brokenness and pain.

God's Word, His instruction manual, is the direction needed in order to fulfill our hope. And though God's Word sometimes seems to include unclear instructions or gray areas, it does not. The areas *we* define as gray or unclear are those we wish to conveniently tuck away or not apply to our lives, even though we know deep within that those particular instructions are what could inevitably set us free from our pain. But sometimes in the attempt to free ourselves, we become overwhelmed and decide it is much simpler to give up altogether.

We are guilty of grappling with God's instructions. We falter in maintaining obedience because we are still of the opinion that *our* way is the best way, the easiest way. Because of that prideful thought, we choose which parts of God's Word we will adhere to, thus falling back into the original state of decline we initially arrived in, at His feet.

In order that we might begin to live obediently by following His blessed instruction manual, we must initiate living an effectual relationship with Jesus Christ. In this relationship, we must draw close to Him in order to receive the much-needed strength and guidance so that the symptoms of brokenness, rejection and pain in our lives might be eliminated or, at the very least, alleviated and more manageable.

Forgive as the Lord forgave you. – Colossians 3:13

I always understood forgiving and being forgiven as two very different concepts—one seemingly much easier than the other. When we ask to be forgiven as the result of a truly penitent heart, we know undoubtedly that God grants us our request. In asking to be forgiven, we ourselves lay claim to the sin offense against God. We also know that we control our turning away from the wickedness for which we asked to be forgiven.

On the other hand, I considered God's most difficult request—to forgive another, an attempted struggle. Granting someone forgiveness made me feel as if I had let my guard down and in doing so, I felt I was a weak person. It was never the actual act or offense that caused me to become frozen in a state of unwillingness to forgive, but rather the persistent pain caused by the act or offense. The act is over within minutes, but the pain can potentially linger for an indefinite amount of time.

I also felt that I could not be guaranteed that the one I'd forgiven wouldn't commit the very same hurt against me in the future. I accepted that the person had made a mistake, but somehow that acknowledgement seemed to open the door for me to have to grant them another forgiveness in the future for the very same hurt. And I felt that this repetitive forgiveness proved somehow that I condoned their actions.

My way of thinking, my reasoning concerning the requirement to forgive others was so poorly understood. The forgiveness I was granting had *nothing* to do with the one being forgiven. I had no control over their choice to continue in their offenses. My forgiveness was all about my life emulating the life of Christ.

How could I possibly continue in this renovation of my soul with unforgiveness in my heart? Unforgiveness and God's love cannot occupy the same space, just as light and darkness cannot occupy the same space. Possessing God's love is both the foundation upon which all Christlike character is built and the enabling power to forgive others.

It is spiritually impossible to put God's Word in my heart and vehemently adhere to it if I don't possess God's love. And in choosing not to forgive, for whatever reason, I am choosing not to exercise the love of Christ. His love is the foundation upon which *all* spiritual renovation is constructed. Without the love of Christ, I cannot even begin to emulate Him. And in my negligence to forgive, I serve only to bring shame to His name while simultaneously failing to glorify Him.

During prayer, I began to speak the names of those I'd chosen not to forgive in my life. I confessed to Christ the hurt they had caused me and that I had carried it for far too long. I knew I still carried unforgiveness in my heart, not because the hurt they caused was at the forefront of my mind. But, only in the course of everyday life were comments made or certain events occurred that would unexpectedly cause my heart to skip a beat as I suddenly recalled the pain caused by those who had hurt me.

The list of those I hadn't forgiven wasn't long, but I felt confident that I had included everyone until I had the strangest dream one night. My youngest daughter was in the dream with me and we were driving in what appeared to be a small neighborhood. Suddenly, out of nowhere, an adult woman and her young adult daughter appeared in the dream. We stopped to speak, but not because they flagged us down or because we hadn't seen them in so long and wished to touch base with them. I never saw the face of the mother or even the daughter. Her daughter talked with my daughter as the mother began conversing with me. I remember them telling us, oddly enough, about some food they had recently eaten that they really enjoyed. I thought this odd not only because it was the only part of the conversation with them that I could remember, but it also didn't seem to fit into the dream. But I do know that if God is the source of a particular dream, every piece and part—the words spoken, the people included, the objects observed, and the colors beheld—undoubtedly hold some kind of spiritual significance.

I woke up and had breakfast the next morning—the dream far from my mind. As I was making my morning coffee, the dream unanticipatedly came to mind and I thought to myself what a really bizarre dream it had been. Then I wondered *why* I even had such a dream.

The Holy Spirit answered with the revelation that I hadn't forgiven the adult female in the dream and though I never saw her face, I instantly knew who it was. I cried uncontrollably as I realized the unequivocal love God has for me. So much so that He had reminded me of a person I needed to forgive that I'd completely forgotten. Had He not reminded me; I would have unknowingly harbored unforgiveness in my heart. In doing so, that unforgiveness would have halted my obedience altogether.

It was days, maybe even weeks, before I came to understand the significance of the food she had mentioned in the dream. "My food," said Jesus, "is to do the will of Him who sent Me and to finish His work" (John 4:34). Just as food is the sustenance of our earthly life, our spiritual sustenance thrives on living the will of God. His will for me was to forgive, and forgiveness is living obediently. In forgiving her, I was able to continue in the will of my Father.

A large part of our obedience requires us to learn to trust in the Lord as we continue in His will. A portion of this trust is giving Him our pain when others hurt us. When we surrender the entirety of such a burden, Christ obligingly lends His aid. I don't know that the pain ever fully goes away, but I do know that if it does, the memory of it will always remain. And for those whose hurt is still as painful as the day it happened, with Christ, that pain will eventually become bearable then manageable then hopefully a distant memory. Once that happens, we can once again begin to live a life filled with godly purpose and joy.

But how often do we give up altogether the pursuit of a life filled with godly purpose and joy when we fail to live obediently? Several years ago, I began having trouble during my weight training—both my right hand and right elbow would begin to throb with pain when I increased the weight beyond a certain point. I spoke with an avid weight lifter who suggested that I continue to lift the heaviest weight that didn't cause pain while attempting to increase the number of repetitions. He explained to me that the increased repetitions would tone muscle just as well while still building the strength I intended.

Three years later, the Holy Spirit quickened that very conversation to mind one evening while I was finishing up my toning exercises. He first reminded me that in whatever we're learning to do or become is at first, very foreign to us. However, the repetition of it affords us the comfort of familiarity.

Secondly, the Holy Spirit reminded me exactly what the avid weight lifter explained to me—by increasing the number of reps while exercising, we build strength as intended. The Holy Spirit explained how *living obedience* is analogous to the *repetition* of toning exercises. The more we practice submission in obedience to the will of God, subsequently, the more comfortable and natural it becomes, almost involuntary. And in the continued practice, we become stronger and more skilled in walking obediently as God intended thus choosing the continued pursuit of a life filled with godly purpose and joy.

Much-Needed Prayer

Do not be anxious about anything, but in everything, by prayer and petition, with thanksgiving, present your requests to God. – Philippians 4:6

Then Jesus told His disciples a parable to show them that they should always pray and not give up. – Luke 18:1

And pray in the Spirit on all occasions with all kinds of prayers and requests. – Ephesians 6:18

Our repetitive choice to live obediently before Christ affords us comfort in a once-foreign environment. The more we practice submission, the more obedience becomes a natural way of life. Prayer is the prime constituent responsible for such obedience. And the more we pray, the more natural our conversation with Jesus becomes. The regularity with which we seek Christ strengthens our relationship with Him while exposing our newly blooming dutiful heart.

Initially, I needed prayer in my life that I might not continue in the one-and-done mentality which, obviously, had proven to be ineffectual. I had for far too long lived under

One and Done

the false pretense that living as a Christian required nothing of myself. To this day, I cannot understand how I could have ever reasonably reached such a distorted conclusion.

I was far more obedient to following the instruction manuals guidance regarding the necessary upkeep of the purchases I'd made than I was to the Word of God. I never considered obedience the fundamental element of Christianity. I deceivingly convinced myself that had I understood that the Bible is the necessary instruction manual needed to spiritually assemble me, I would have been more inclined to read it.

At first, I found it most challenging to pray. I would designate a specific time each day to pray but out of the blue and conveniently for me, a much more "pressing" issue would require my time. To avoid prayer, I readily convinced myself that these rather trifling issues were pressing. In actuality, these so-called issues never amounted to a hill of beans. More often than not, the most influential reason I did not pray was the ludicrous nonsense I allowed myself to believe. The thoughts that played over and over in my mind included: I wasn't holy enough to pray a holy prayer, the needs in my life were really of no consequence and lastly, I was simply a bother to God. The truth was I could not begin to pray until I *forced* myself to shut down such degrading and debasing thoughts which made me feel defeated before I had even begun. Though I didn't know it at the time, the culprit who served as the origin of such thoughts was none other than the enemy himself. Finally, I decided I could no longer devise some sort of plan in order to create a most opportune time to pray. I just had to thrust myself into it. So, whenever I could devote even a few spare minutes during the day to pray, I was there before the face of God.

I decided beforehand to set only two goals for my prayer time that I considered reasonable, simple and attainable. My first goal was to pray every single day regardless of the unforeseen, sudden circumstances of daily life that came my way. In an attempt to meet this first goal, I initially thought it wise to wait for the house to be empty. Weekdays were easy because the kids were at school and on those weekdays when my husband wasn't working, he'd very happily occupy his time running enjoyable yet insignificant errands.

I chose to pray when no one else was home for two very meaningful reasons. First, when the kids were home, there were undoubtedly, endless interruptions which would have frustrated me. And frustration served as an easy enough excuse to stop any attempt to pray for the entire day.

Secondly, I assumed that if my husband had known I was praying daily, he would have this unwarranted expectancy of immediate change in me. I knew, unlike him, that change only ever happens over a period of time, but I felt if I had to explain this to him, he might've innocently misconstrued my explanation as an excuse not to change. So, to avoid this altogether, I didn't pray when he was home.

My second reasonable and attainable goal was to pray no less than three minutes each day. Yes, I said only three minutes. But those three minutes seemed an eternity when I first began praying. A defined minimum amount of time would force me to be engaged in prayer for that designated time frame.

Initially, this newfound habit in my life made me feel awkward; I found it difficult to speak with Jesus. So, as a result, my first many, many prayers were filled solely with worship. I felt comfortable in praising the King of kings. I felt joy and peace in my worship of Him and I never tired of praising Him. Eventually, my worship preceded my conversation with Jesus—comfortable, much-needed conversation. It turned out I didn't have to "sound" holy. How does one even sound holy, anyway? No one but Jesus heard me praying, so it certainly wasn't a requirement. I just needed to pour out my heart before Jesus. I needed to unburden myself and in doing so, I was giving it to Jesus.

I began to understand that prayer was about so much more than just what I needed to ask Jesus to do in my life. In this unburdening, I began to understand an all too often unmentioned purpose in the power of prayer; it is healing and therapeutic for the soul! It was only in sharing the concerns and burdens in my life that I was unknowingly giving the Lord *control* over my life. I was actually admitting to Him that despite all my so-called knowledge and know-how to handle certain situations, in reality I possessed *no* such knowledge and know-how. I was finally recognizing the need for Him to bear the burdens I could no longer bear alone.

Allowing God to take over brings great peace. This "giving it all to God" is not yet perfected in me, but there is hope. I know that though I'm not growing by leaps and bounds in relinquishing all burdens . . . I. Am. Growing. This growing signifies progress and reminds me that I'm not spiritually stagnant. It reminds me just how far I've come from that person who once believed the ludicrous, nonsensical lies of the enemy and how that forced me to purposely dodge prayer. I've reached a point in my life where I simply *must* find time to slip away to talk with my Heavenly Father. I must. I yearn to be in His presence. I long to become adept in hearing Him speak to me. In longing to be in His presence, I lose all track of time. And that initial goal—pray at least three minutes—is so funny to me now because as I get wrapped up in conversation with Christ, I greatly exceed that initial three-minute goal.

Because We Love

If you love Me, you will obey what I command.
– John 14:15

Jesus replied, "If anyone loves me, he will obey my teaching. My Father will love him, and we will come to him and make our home with him. He who does not love me will not obey my teaching." – John 14:23-24

Prayer is obedience. Obedience is prayer. In choosing disobedience, we have essentially come to the conclusion that we know a better way, a faster way, a wiser way and a less self-sacrificing way than the obedience that is asked of us. We have arrived at this senseless conclusion because we seek convenience in our lives. This present conclusion fails to recall past consequences that disobedience generated.

We have unreasonably convinced ourselves that disobedience will somehow create for us a newfound, promising opportunity that obedience could not have otherwise provided. We'd rather live having taken our chance on disobedience than live feeling shortchanged by living obedience. We legitimize our irrational thinking based on our survival of the consequences of our disobedience.

Disobedience will always lead to a state of emotional, physical and/or spiritual suffering of some kind. It leads to either an immediate consequence or a delayed consequence—delayed in that it *later* presents itself the moment we *think* we have escaped retribution. But it is always the case that disobedience is the promised delivery of something unwanted—something we've chosen to do that is now too late to take back and to choose obedience instead. Our repeated disobedience reflects our indisputable egocentric and prideful attitude. Though this far we have managed to survive the consequences of disobediences, be assured the day will come when we are consumed by a consequence.

In choosing obedience, we choose love. In our obedience to God's Word, our love for Him is revealed. I always tell God how very much I love Him. And while those three words never seem to capture the depth of my love for Him, He is nonetheless fully aware. In keeping His word, we practice obedience thus *proving* that our love for Him is more than a mere proclamation— "If anyone *loves* Me, he will *obey* My teaching" (John 14:23, author emphasis). Our actions always speak louder than our words (See 1 John 3:18.)

As toddlers, my children found boundless excitement in pleasing my husband and me because when they did what was asked of them, we'd make a big to-do of it. At times, their obedience deserved a bonus in the form of stickers and candy treats. This was especially true when my children were learning to potty train.

One and Done

But even as adults, my children still love to share their achievements, whether scholarly or career-oriented. In knowing they've always been held to a certain standard in all that they do, they share their joy with us in accomplishing and even exceeding those standards. I believe it is because my husband and I have always acknowledged their accomplishments with joyful praise.

At report card time, we as parents are concerned about the letter grades, but the comment section of the report card always meant so much more to me. Their letter grades were a reflection of their obedience out of love for their parents, but the comment section was a reflection of the love and self-worth they possessed for themselves. These comments from their teachers were what separated them from their peers. These comments spoke to their character and their choices and they defined and supported who they were and who, exactly, they chose to stand for.

I am of the opinion that God is making comments in the comment section of our earthly "report card." As Christians, we are held to a higher standard and our adherence to that standard is reflected in our obedience.

I want my comment section to be filled with the same comments I've seen in the past on the report cards of my children. These comments document that I have been joyfully obeying His teachings:

> A positive LEADER: seeks to love like He loves, to forgive as He forgives, to walk as He walks
> CONSCIENTIOUS student: makes godly choices over good choices. Consults with Him in all things knowing that:
  - When I ask, He hears.
  - When I cry, He sees.
  - When I feel empty, He fills the vacancy.
  - When I am lonely, He comes alongside me.
  - When I am weak, He is strong.
  - When there is trouble, He is the answer.
> PLEASURE to have in class: strives for obedience.

Our comment section should reflect our most earnest desire to live obediently before our Heavenly Father out of love. Initially, our attempted obedience is something we felt we *had* to do in choosing to live for our King. But in our loving pursuit of Him and all that He longs to do in our lives, we no longer conceive the fulfillment of our obedience as obedience. Instead, we consider it a blessed way of life in which we *joyfully choose* to abide. Our obedience substantiates the depth of our love for Him. "He who does not love me will not obey my teaching" (John 14:24).

One and Done

Bringing Your Sight Into Focus

Let your eyes look straight ahead, fix your gaze directly before you. – Proverbs 4:25

How much time do we lose longing for the yesterdays in our lives? In looking back, we yearn to relive a special moment or to somehow make a remorseful moment right. In looking back, we fail to let our eyes look straight ahead. And in looking ahead, the new day brings the promise of yet another special moment and yet another opportunity to live an unremorseful moment.

Initially, the sole reason my husband attended college was to play baseball on a scholarship. Obtaining a bachelor's degree, secondary to playing ball, was something he had to do in order to cash in the scholarship he had received. It wasn't until the end of his sophomore year that he realized the prospect of becoming a professional ball player was slim to none— leaning more heavily towards none. He decided it was time to grow up and face reality. He declared a major in Criminal Justice only because he thought it sounded interesting enough to hold his attention long enough to finish his degree.

In this particular major, there was one professor who taught multiple classes due to both his abundance of knowledge in the criminal justice field and his own personal experiences which provided invaluable insight to his scholarly lessons as well as life itself. One such benefit of his personal experiences was his longtime friendship with an F.B.I. agent who offered to speak to the professor's college students, as he would be in town. Appointed by God, the exact date and time the agent was available coincided with the date, time *and* semester my husband would be taking this particular course.

The day the agent spoke in class, a result of God's divine appointment, my husband discovered his choice career. He earned his bachelor's degree in Criminal Justice then took the police exam. Twenty-five years later, he has never regretted that decision he made so long ago.

While in the police academy, he trained with the gun that he would eventually be issued when sworn in as an officer. However, his problem was his inability to hit the target as needed in order to receive a passing grade. So, he sought additional training from the range instructor. The instructor explained three very critical steps my husband must practice to ensure the accuracy needed in hitting the target.

First, the instructor noticed my husband closing his dominant eye as he engaged the trigger and as the tension in the trigger grew taut, my husband voluntarily jerked the gun upward in anticipation of the gun firing. The instructor told him to consciously force that eye to remain open while fixating his finger on the trigger, which would prevent him from jerking the gun upward and missing the target.

Second, the instructor warned him not to allow the other shooters on the line, those in his peripheral vision, to distract him from keeping his eye on the target.

Last, he told him to focus on the front sight *nearer* the target.

The suggested precepts to practice as stated by the range instructor are the very same precepts God would want believers to follow in order to successfully apply Proverbs 4:25 to our lives.

Firstly, just as my husband consciously forced himself to control both his dominant eye and the movement of his hand, we as Christians must train ourselves to control our thoughts and actions in order to maintain a state of obedience. God longs for us to hit the target of living obediently before Him. One way to successfully accomplish this is by not looking back on our past. Looking back can be suggestive of a longing for those days—a time when we felt comfortable because we lived for ourselves. The life we led because of the choices we made in the past, should serve solely as life lessons. The *past* should promote and allow a *present* joyful reflection of our growth. The past should be a reminder that certain of our decisions did not reflect a salvational life—a life that should have focused on Jesus Christ and not on ourselves.

Secondly, in looking straight ahead, we unmistakably notice that our peripheral vision is still engaged. Peripheral vision is defined as "a part of vision that occurs *outside* the *center* of my gaze"[1] (author emphasis). Anything outside the center of our gaze is a distraction. These distractions include the situations and people *outside* the spiritual domain that serve only to deter our focus from the *center*. "Then I saw a Lamb, looking as if it had been slain, standing in the center of the throne" (Revelation 5:6). As we commit to the lifelong effort to ignore what lies within our peripheral vision, we are choosing to focus on what lies at the center—Christ Jesus, Himself. We must continue to look straight ahead, ever aware of the potential sinful downfall we are subjected to by our peripheral vision.

Last, fixing our gaze before us, we see clearly as opposed to the strenuous attempt to see far beyond what is right before us. In trying to look far beyond, our vision is blurred and the road appears unending. But, as we are moving while looking right before us, we can confidently step into the things of God little by little. They are achievable steps securely taken without fear of the unending and daunting road that lies before us. As our gaze remains directly fixed on who is at the center, we are assured we will hit the target of living obediently.

I like to think this small growth in obedience, stepping into the commands of God little by little, ensures permanency.

It's like a baby learning to walk; he naturally goes through a series of developmental stages. Within each stage, extraordinary skills are gained that ultimately lead to the skilled perfection of walking. Some of the same invaluable qualities produced in the toddler's developmental stages of walking overlap the qualities gained in learning to walk obediently before Christ. They are alike in that we gained mental stamina in the face of numerous failed attempts. Furthermore, as an encouraging loved one is ever before the toddler, our Lord is ever before us encouraging us. The mental stamina coupled with encouragement are vital, key ingredients that foster the numerous attempts needed to finally achieve the required familiarity with the task that leads to the newfound skill.

Caution: Road Curves Ahead

Do not swerve to the right or the left. – Proverbs 4:27

This caution sign—road curves ahead, is a forewarning to travelers to use extra caution in maneuvering a particular roadway. Curvy roads prevent us from seeing what lies directly ahead. This is especially true of roads tucked away in mountainous regions or roads lined and populated with dense, mature trees. When we lose that crucial, much-needed visibility, we must all the more heed the speed limit and cautionary signs as we travel these treacherous roads.

Whether we've voluntarily taken this road or we were forced to take it as there were no alternative routes, we are still aware of the latent problems as we have been forewarned by the caution sign.

God's Word is chock-full of caution signs. And whether we've made a choice or life has unexpectedly dealt us an inauspicious situation, we have the blessed Word of God to steer us out of dangers, toils and snares. In our choice to adhere to His wisdom, we choose not to suddenly veer off course. The off-course journey is neither endorsed by our Heavenly Father nor equipped with directional and cautionary signs. However, if we do veer off course, we must at the very first opportunity steer ourselves back onto the road that is filled with forewarning signs given by God that serve to prosper our way.

It is most advantageous to equip ourselves with blinders, so to speak, just as a jockey forcibly equips a racehorse. Because of the placement of their eyes, every horse is naturally attentive to what is taking place both beside him and behind him. The blinders forcibly remove the distraction of the other horses.

As we run the course of life, we too, are naturally attentive to all that is taking place around us. But by way of absorbing the Word of God, we are ever advancing our spiritual renovation. As the Word of God serves as our blinders, we are likely to stay the God-intended course.

Proverbs 4:27 serves as just one of God's abundant cautionary signs. As God is not a dictator, He does not force us to adhere to His Word. However, in choosing not to swerve to the right or to the left, we are trusting the precept taught. In veering off course, we not only disappoint ourselves in our desire to be obedient, but we also incite much unwanted havoc and we seriously delay God's plan for our lives. Remember always, "let us throw off everything that hinders and the sin that so easily entangles" (See Hebrews 12:1.)

Where We Start

Trust in the Lord with all your heart and lean not on your own understanding. – Proverbs 3:5

The direction of the road chosen is not a prerequisite to the gift of life's indelible lessons. We are frequently afforded opportunities to utilize a new, intended, fond wisdom to grow us into godlier people. We'd be wise to employ the immediate, present knowledge learned, to our future life choices regardless of how frequent or infrequent the opportunity arises to do so.

However, in those cases when we do veer off course, we have the privilege to take advantage of the availability of life's lessons. But in taking that chance, we are never guaranteed that we will return to the road where Christ intended for us to be. We should therefore, first, make the godly choice not to swerve to the right or to the left. In choosing not to swerve, we can ever focus on Christ at the center thus indisputably promoting our obedience.

As we are learning to trust in the Lord, it eventually becomes apparent that the route taken offered invaluable knowledge that, if implemented, could serve as a lesson to grow us into godlier people. For so long, I misunderstood the application of Scripture in my life. I thought it was applicable to a situation only *after* the situation required some type of special attention. And by that point, I had become so furious with the problem that I neglected to walk away with the lesson.

The majority of the time, *I* was the reason the situation had even become a problem because I was not seeking God in my life, let alone His will for my life. In my mind it seemed rational to take care of the problems that I, alone, had caused. I always rationalized that the choices I had made were the reason I ended up in such precarious situations. The only right thing to do, it seemed, was to get myself out of them. What I missed entirely concerning the purpose of any Scripture was if I had trusted in the Lord *at first* by applying His Word, perhaps I wouldn't have ended up in the problem to begin with—or if the problem still persisted, perhaps the severity of it would not have.

Trusting in the Lord *is* trusting in His commands. It's where we *start*. It's not an afterthought. Our spirit wars against the flesh in that, though we understand His ways are not our ways (See Isaiah 55:8), we refuse to acknowledge that they are, in fact, always better.

Our refusal to institute God's command to trust in Him could be for any number of reasons; one of which may include our inability to comprehend how trusting in His ways are always beneficial to our lives. For example, the Lord commands that we tithe. We may concede that tithing works in the lives of others. But as is often the case with so many of God's commands, it's easy to stand back and gaze upon the lives of others and convince ourselves that what works for others just won't work for us.

In actuality, however, we're not concerned with whether it would really work in our lives or not. We don't really give any thought to that. What we shamefully withhold is the *real* reason we offer excuses for the commands that we claim just won't work for us. It is because we pick and choose from amongst God's commands only those that *conveniently* work in our lives, without disrupting our life as we currently know it.

Obedience is not the promise of a worry-free, problem-free life. Rather, obedience is our acknowledgement of the promises He's made for our lives. And in choosing disobedience, we nullify these promises available to us.

Nothing, absolutely nothing with God is an afterthought (See Isaiah 46:10.) And because of this, as we have the mind of Christ (See 1 Corinthians 2:16.), nothing should be an afterthought for us. His request to trust in Him should be right where we start at the beginning of each new dawn, in each situation. As we begin to give Him all of us, He begins to unleash, little by little, all of Him. As we live to trust in Him, we invite all the promises of God into our obedient lives while glorifying Him.

Ever Thankful

It is apparent that as God's commands become our customary way of life, our loved ones can become the recipient of blessings for our obedience. For me, if this were the *only* promise gained in following His commands, it would definitely be the only encouragement I'd ever need to live all my days obediently.

I am ever thankful for the understanding that trusting in the Lord must always be the starting point of each and every day. I entrust to Christ the life my children lead in that I cast all my care upon Him regarding the lives of my children (See 1 Peter 5:7, KJV.) In one such particular incident, both my daughter and I reaped a most memorable and uplifting blessing in our lives as the result of lifting my hands to Him for the lives of my children (See Lamentations 2:19.)

One and Done

My daughter dated what appeared to be a nice young boy. He dressed appropriately, played sports in school and always went out of his way to engage in conversation with my husband and me. In getting to know one another in the first six months of their relationship, they genuinely seemed to enjoy each other's company. But after the first six months, my daughter's personality changed—the joy she once radiated and the smile she once offered so frequently was suddenly gone. The changes, seemingly small to some, were huge red flags to me and of great concern. As always, I would cast this care upon the Lord. I would specifically request Him not to allow anyone to rob her of her most beautiful attributes both spiritually and physically.

These personality changes weren't a daily occurrence, so I convinced myself that if her smile and joy returned for even a few consecutive days or even here and there, it meant that all was somehow well again. In those moments, I decided to recuse myself from her personal affairs.

But as time endured, I lost hope that she would permanently return to her old self. As any loving and attentive parent would do, I confronted her numerous times. Most times she attributed her less-than-normal self to difficulty with one particular class and exhaustion from the required early morning tutoring. Other times, she explained that she and her boyfriend had a disagreement. This too didn't seem abnormal as all new relationships suffer growing pains. Though I accepted her reasoning face to face, as a Christian filled with the Holy Spirit and as a loving mom, I discerned that something was still just not right. All the while I continued in prayer. Just because we cast our cares upon Him doesn't mean that prayer begins and ends with such words. Even though Christ knows our heart, we still divulge our deepest desires concerning the lives of our children.

As my own children fall in and out of relationships, I ask the Lord to help them and me recognize a situation that could potentially become harmful to them—whether with friends or someone they are dating. I then ask the Lord to help them tap into the mighty attributes of being bold and stouthearted—attributes He's *already* equipped them with as this Scripture is past tense, "I have *made* you bold and stouthearted" (Psalm 138:3, author emphasis). These attributes would be needed to sever any harmful relationship.

One evening as I watched television, my daughter walked into the room and began to tell me about her visit with a friend she hadn't seen in months. This conversation conveniently flowed into the opportunity to inquire about how things were with her and this boy she was dating.

She told me the relationship was not good. She then very honestly told me that she could not share with me the reasons it had turned sour. Personally, I did not care as to *why* it had turned sour. My preeminent concern was that in his ongoing successful emotional abuse and spiritual abuse, proven by the absence of her smile and joy, was he not also physically abusing her?

As she continued in conversation, I respectfully kept quiet, though I thought of a million questions I needed to ask. But before I asked her, I paused to think for a few seconds because I didn't want to stifle the conversation she had so willingly begun. I carefully chose the one question I thought was most relevant to the topic at hand. I asked her if she thought she knew me well enough to know how *I* would handle the affairs of this relationship if *I* were in her shoes. She told me she most definitely knew how I'd handle the situation. The answer to that question was paramount because sometimes in knowing that another's choice was successful, we can find the strength to make that same choice for ourselves.

My daughter explained to me that she thought the boy she was dating would eventually change, though she didn't specify to me the change she thought he needed. I then asked the one question whose answer could quite possibly reveal one's acknowledgement of the need to change—though an affirmative answer is not a guarantee that change will commence. Sometimes, a momentary affirmative answer is nothing more than a manipulative show of feigned guilt. I asked her if he *ever* apologized to her for *anything* of his *own* initiative. She unhesitatingly answered with an emphatic no. She disclosed the truth that he had only ever apologized as a result of her indifference towards him.

I explained that those who never identify themselves as the culprit in any problem, in any relationship, are most certainly not headed towards change. Change requires self-reflection—the willingness to step back from oneself, analyze the situation and humbly take ownership for their own defective contributions to the relationship. Apologies from those who speak them only as a result of the cold shoulder are not looking to change; they are simply the culprit's attempt to draw the one they've offended back into the relationship. I further explained that it wasn't her responsibility to change anyone and that waiting for something that might never happen is a loss of valuable time.

My daughter abruptly rose from her chair and told me she loved me. That was it—no questions were asked and no comments were made about all that was spoken between us. She simply left the room. I wondered whether I had offended her, but I also knew it was my duty as a Christian mother to guide her as best I knew how and to be honest with her in everything.

One and Done

A couple days had gone by and faithfully, every day, I asked how things were going. She'd nonchalantly reply that things were good—oh, but how I longed to delve into the nitty gritty of what was really happening after we had our discussion.

One day after school, her dad mentioned to her that her boyfriend texted him about purchasing mulch for a fundraiser program at school for the baseball team. She replied, surprisingly, unemotionally and unstirred that she didn't know to whom her dad was referring since she currently had no boyfriend.

My husband and I exchanged glances. We were shocked, bewildered, flabbergasted and absolutely speechless. Life, once again, was really and truly going good for her. As the days passed, bit by bit, she shared the verbal and emotional abuse she had tolerated. She had dated him for only fifteen months and could honestly admit that only the first six months were pleasant. His words brought destruction and death, not encouragement and life. Eventually, he would have emptied her of every ounce of joy she radiated and the smiles she possessed by inhumanely crushing her spirit with intimidation and contempt.

I explained to her that no human being should tolerate such abusive treatment. I reminded her to never forget to cause her faith to rest in someone bigger than her problems.

Only and especially because she is a child of the King, He will always protect her from those who malign her. She knows that as Christ is able to deliver her, she does in fact, have the courage to pursue a better life. I told her how easily verbal abuse becomes physical abuse and then she spoke these words to me: "Thank you for listening to me that night. Thank you for encouraging me in ways you were not even aware of. In knowing how *you'd* respond, I found the strength to respond in the very same way."

As a result of that situation with my daughter, it became apparent to me that in following God's commands, our loved ones reap the blessings of our obedience. I had faithfully and fully given it all to God. So much could have gone awry as a result of that breakup. I thought of those who fall into depression or even commit suicide when a relationship fails.

In looking back on that day when she thanked me for helping her find the strength to respond as I would have, I realized her words were misdirected. They should have been spoken directly to Christ Jesus. You see, the magnitude of the blessing, all that was restored, was *Christ's* faithfulness in answering my prayer that He would help her tap into her boldness and stoutheartedness and not allow her beautiful attributes to be stolen. That blessing, to this day, has had an unforgettable impact on both of our lives.

Cleanliness

First clean the inside of the cup and dish, and then the outside also will be clean. – Matthew 23:26

It is a necessity that the dishes used to serve our food possess a sanitary clean. For some, the easiest way to achieve this is the convenient use of a dishwasher. When loading a dishwasher, it is of utmost importance that deep dishes be turned upside down on the dishwasher racks to allow the surfaces with food remnants to directly face the sprayers. As the water fills the sprayers, the force created ensures the cleanliness of the dish.

As Christians, we must purposely position ourselves in the things of God so that our deepest parts, once filled with sin, become a godly clean. As we fill our minds with the boundaries and precepts of God, we begin the process of internal cleansing.

As Christians, our every final word and action is a direct result of an *initial* incoming thought. Everything we say and every choice we make—whether good or bad—originates in the mind (See Matthew 15:19.) The very moment we begin to entertain a thought is the very moment we begin to weave that thought into our hearts. The moment we act upon those thoughts in our heart is the very moment they have become ingrained in us. Once ingrained, it is not easy to turn from.

Imagine that our thoughts are like words strewn across a blackboard. We can choose, quite easily at first, to leave them there or to simply erase them. If we choose to allow those thoughts to remain on the blackboard of our mind, for whatever reason, then we've already begun to entertain those thoughts. It is at this point that the thoughts are now being woven into our hearts. Once woven, but with much greater difficulty, we can *still* choose to turn from them, but sometimes the struggle is so great, we exhaust our every effort and finally give in.

But obviously, those thoughts carried out cannot be erased or undone. The act is proof that what started as an initial thought can become ingrained. An initial thought that is repeatedly entertained and now finally woven into the heart will undoubtedly and unfailingly, manifest itself outwardly. We can with the greatest effort and most determined labor try not to repeat the sinful act which is ingrained—and while it might work sometimes, for the most part, what we are inwardly will repeatedly and accurately be reflected outwardly.

Let's take for instance the following example. Couple A befriended couple B. Both the husband and the wife of couple B possessed runway model looks, earned ivy league educations, drove pricey cars, and maintained the upper income to support such a comfortable lifestyle.

From the beginning of their friendship, the wife of couple A, Joan, while only periodically, would find herself comparing the things she and her husband had to the things couple B had: couple B drove more expensive vehicles, their home had been decorated by a professional, and they had a pool house to accompany their backyard pool.

Eventually, Joan started to compare herself more specifically to the wife of couple B, Beatrice. Joan felt that Beatrice's education was superior to her own as Beatrice had attended an ivy league institution and while Beatrice carried the title of a high-ranking position in her employment, Joan remained a homemaker. To top it off, not only was Beatrice stunning to look at, she was incredibly kind.

Joan's envy gnawed at her. She convinced herself that she was inferior to Beatrice. This inferiority compulsion generated hateful thoughts toward Beatrice. A once, only intermittent, tease of envy in her thoughts, seemingly overnight took up woven residency in her heart. And woven in her heart, once outwardly manifested, was now ingrained. Joan's curt replies abruptly ended the beginning of any conversation Beatrice initiated. As time moved on, and Joan's loathsome attitude toward Beatrice lingered, their friendship ended.

We render ourselves ineffective to position ourselves in the things of God if we don't possess the knowledge to identify what the things of God are. God's Word is the sole effective, distinguishable source teaching us what to turn from and what to lean into. In reading the Word of God, we are empowered to pray the Word of God, thereby enabling us to live the Word of God, consequently causing us to be positioned in the things of God.

The only way to ensure a godly cleanliness is to purposely bathe ourselves in the things of God so that we can keep clean the inside of our cup and dish—our mind and heart. In the same way that a dishwasher renders a sanitary clean by the forceful spray of water, "the washing with water *through the word*" renders a pure clean (Ephesians 5:26, author emphasis). As we read His Word daily, God's love and commandments become our initial incoming thoughts while fervent prayer begins to weave much contemplated Scripture into our hearts. It is only then that our outward display of God's love and precepts will accurately reveal what has become ingrained in us.

In reading the Word of God, we educate ourselves in the person of Jesus Christ and the precepts He taught that we are expected to live by. As these precepts and boundaries are woven into our hearts, they serve further to filter incoming thoughts engendered by the outside world. Those thoughts that align themselves with the Word are acceptable to entertain. As life dictates, our responses will accurately reflect the things of God.

CHAPTER FIVE

Vile

Vile is the perverse that begets a curse.

Everything that is vile (evil, shameful, vicious, disgraceful, deceitful) is perverse thus causing one to deviate from what is right and good and honorable, in turn igniting a curse such as misfortune, or bane. Vile is not only that which can be seen, but vile also includes all that is spoken, heard, or thought. Whether in the presence of others or alone, whether we commit the vile deed or we subject ourselves to the vile deeds of others, we alone are responsible for stepping outside what is right and good. And in habitually stepping outside of what is right and good, we voluntarily step outside the ordinances of God and in doing so, it is vile sin. The moment anything vile gains entry into our lives is the moment a curse begins.

We have this preconceived misunderstanding that vile can only legitimately accompany the worst of sin. It is not only a vain attempt, but also erroneous, to somehow rank sin based upon some sort of varying "degrees" of its severity. The bottom line is—all repeated sin is vile. Our concentration should remain focused on the certainty of Scripture: when we know the right and the good that we should be doing, yet make a conscious choice not to do it, that's sin (See James 4:17.) Additionally, all sin, irrespective of *what* sin is committed, separates us from God (See Isaiah 59:2.) Eventually, repeated sin begets a curse such as misfortune, adversity or trouble. In order to avoid such ruin, it is critical that we steer clear of everything that is vile.

Seen and Unseen

I will set before my eyes no vile thing. – Psalm 101:3

We've all heard the well-known adage, *look but don't touch.* The adage is often popular among those who deludingly think that innocence can be maintained in only looking. Yet, God specifically tells us in no uncertain terms not to set before our *eyes* anything that is vile. He doesn't give us clearance to look then forewarn us not to touch. Why? He knows that our eyes are the entryway for the creation of sinful thoughts. Looking is the fuel needed to start the thought process, and sinful thoughts lead to sinful actions. We do not remain guiltless in our premeditated urge to unremittingly set the vile before our eyes. The *unseen* evil desire subsequently ignites the sin that *is* seen.

One such example of an unseen desire is lust. According to Vine's Complete Expository Dictionary, lust "refers to those evil desires ready to express themselves in bodily action" (Thomas Nelson, 1984). An evil lustful desire isn't simply pulled from the air. Our eyes are the gateway by which certain evil desires begin to stir: "for everything in the world—the cravings of sinful man, the lust of his eyes." (See 1 John 2:16.)

Consider Ephesians 2:3 which says, "gratifying the cravings of our sinful nature and *following* its *desires* and *thoughts*" (author emphasis). It is clearly understood from this passage that we are sinners by nature. Furthermore, it is understood that the unseen evil thoughts and the unseen evil desires are triggered by outside sin. These thoughts and desires serve as the conduit for the sin which is seen and heard. Additionally, Matthew 15:19 tells us, "for out of the heart come evil thoughts." The resulting, observable sin is a manifestation of what began as an evil thought influenced by that which is seen.

Christ warns in 2 Corinthians 10:5 that we should "take captive every thought to make it obedient to Christ." Why is Christ teaching to take captive the thought? Because the thought is where the evil desires begin. If we do not know what sin is as defined by God in His Word, then we are not equipped to identify those thoughts that we readily need to seize and make obedient to Christ. As a result, we will suffer great repercussions resulting from the coercing force of an initial mere thought. The thoughts we incessantly dwell on become part of the heart and, in acting upon them, they become not only seen but are now ingrained as well.

We often attempt to somehow categorize sin. This affords us the opportunity to favorably place *ourselves* in a most desirable category. Categories of our choice fondly include "that's not really sin" and "that's sin of a much lesser degree." In categorizing sin, we convince ourselves that our thoughts and actions are okay with God. In our self-restricted knowledge of the Bible, the only sin we aware of, the Ten Commandments, serve as our all-encompassing sin directive.

Our simple common sense could never know *all* that is vile (evil, shameful, deceitful) to God. But as we delve into the Word of God, we are shocked to discover that there is much sin in addition to the Ten Commandments. As we educate ourselves in God's Word, we realize how grateful we are for the discovery of such sin. It is eternally crucial that we familiarize ourselves with God's precepts so that when prompted by the Spirit of the sin we committed, we can seek God's forgiveness and rid ourselves of any potential repeated sin that separates us from the King.

All that is opposite God, who alone defines all that is good and righteous, is evil. All evil is vile. All that is vile is perverse. Proverbs 6:16-19 is a good starting point in understanding what is vile to God:

> There are six things the Lord hates, seven that are detestable to him: haughty eyes, a lying tongue, hands that shed innocent blood, a heart that devises wicked schemes, feet that are quick to rush into evil, a false witness who pours out lies and a man who stirs up dissension among brothers.

Other examples include:

> For from within, out of men's hearts, come evil thoughts, sexual immorality, theft, murder, adultery, greed, malice, deceit, lewdness, envy, slander, arrogance and folly. All these evils come from inside and make a man unclean (Mark 7:21-23).

> But now you must rid yourselves of all such things as these: anger, rage, malice, slander, and filthy language from your lips (Colossians 3:8).

> Put to death, therefore, whatever belongs to your earthly nature: sexual immorality, impurity, lust, evil desires and greed, which is idolatry (Colossians 3:5).

The vileness that men commit invariably begins with incessant vile thoughts. We are held accountable for both the vile acts and the vile thoughts that lead to them. But, are we responsible for setting before our eyes that which would otherwise seem out of our control? The answer is an emphatic yes.

The older my children get, the less time my husband and I have with them. Often, my husband and I take a back seat, understandably, as they are tugged in all different directions in their own lives. In those rare times when we are all together with nowhere to be, it is a blessing—a gift granted by chance, not often enough, that I dearly treasure. And during these rare times, the suggestion to rent a movie isn't uncommon—and I hesitatingly concur.

Movies, in order to generate large audiences, which in turn generate enormous revenues, are full of vile content. The difficult attempt to choose a movie without vile content is nearly impossible—a battle that I frequently find myself losing. These movies do not restrict themselves to adultery, murder, idolatry and lies, just to name a few. The absolute worst for me, personally, is the misappropriation

Vile

of God's name. My instantaneous, physical reaction is to throw my hands over my ears and ask God to forgive me when I hear it.

My first emotional response is anger in that another word could not have been chosen out of the entire English language. My second emotional response is sadness to think how many people are not angered when God's name is profanely used. Obviously, not very many as proven by its repeated use. After repeated use, which is more often than not, I dismiss myself from the movie I'm watching with my family because I refuse to allow all that is vile to sear my conscience. However, I do not share with my children or my husband my reasons for leaving as they are well aware by now it's something the Lord has requested I do. My spiritual censures are not their spiritual censures. I cannot be their conscience, nor do I want to be. When they were young, we spent the majority of our time making our children's choices. We did so hoping that as they grew into adulthood, the choices we once forced would become the choices they presently choose.

This is not to say that we don't offer guidance. In love we most certainly do, whether we are asked or not. One such piece of advice we continue to give is that if they heed our teaching in the beginning, there will be little or no regret in the end. God does not force our hand in any choice we make, so in emulating Him, we do not force their hand in the choices they make. When we force our choices on our children, the only result is resentment. Our hope is that our children discern the prosperity of our own lives as we attempt to live obediently according to the will of God and desire this way of life for themselves.

In their freedom to *choose* godly living, there is permanency. Such permanency is not suggestive of a sinless life, but rather a life that lays claim to the need to be forgiven by the loving grace of Jesus and the power of the Holy Spirit to reinstitute the will of God.

We cannot escape the overload of all that is vile in the world in which we live today, but we can choose to educate ourselves about all that is vile in the sight of God. The choice to educate ourselves reveals our willingness to reject it—whether it's something we see, hear, think or do—with the full understanding that our rejection of such vileness sows the promise of great and awesome benefits in our lives.

Exposure

Men of perverse heart shall be far from me. – Psalm 101:4

It is not by happenstance that the verse above immediately follows, *"I will set before my eyes no vile thing."* Nothing God does is ever by accident. In fact, God already

Vile

has a plan and a purpose in all that He institutes. He is methodical. He is the God that makes known the end from the very beginning.

While the *content* of God's Word is of the utmost preeminence, we should give no less credence to the planned *order* of His Word. First, the succession of this verse substantiates the pathway that anything vile pursues. The eyes are the entryway for ingesting all that is vile. Then the repetitive thoughts maliciously, slowly and numbly weave themselves into the heart (See Matthew 9:4.) So it is then that men of perverse heart have already engaged the consumption of the vileness taken in by the eyes. We now know unequivocally that this person has no standing relationship with God. The vileness that we just witnessed is our forewarning to distance ourselves from such a person.

There is an unwritten, misguided understanding that as Christians it is not godly to distance ourselves from such people . . . that somehow our godly love, in the presence of the ungodly, will begin to stir the hearts of men—so much so that they astonishingly turn from their wickedness. This injudicious understanding could very well serve to lead the *godly* astray (See 2 Corinthians 6:14-15.) Our responsibility as Christians is first to our brethren in Christ and then to the unbeliever who would lead us to interpret his biblical inquiry as an open invitation to share the knowledge of salvation. And at that, we cannot change the heart of man; only God possesses such power.

It is assuring that as adults with a mind of our own that our gathered wisdom, coupled with the security in who we are, prevents us from responding in an ungodly manner to immature peer pressure. In the security of who we are and for whom we stand, we have no fear of being ostracized for walking away from the exposure of any wickedness and sin. As Paul states, "be on your guard so that you may not be carried away by the error of lawless men and fall from your secure position" (2 Peter 3:17). Our children, on the other hand, are not afforded this assurance. Unfortunately, they live daily the potential threat of cruel, inhuman, and sadistic peer pressure. My hope is that my children will choose to steer clear of those that may serve only to lead them astray.

In understanding 1 Corinthians 5:11, "But now I am writing you that you must not associate with anyone who calls himself a brother but is sexually immoral or greedy, an idolater or a slanderer, a drunkard or a swindler. With such a man do not even eat," how much more important is it then to dissociate with those who live lives opposite of Christ. Sometimes, my children are amongst friends who know my children are Christians but mistakenly think that my children should not dissociate themselves from a certain crowd of people for fear the dissociation is not

Vile

Christlike. I explain to my children this misunderstanding is far from the truth.

In allowing themselves to be surrounded with such ungodliness, they are subjecting themselves to a very volatile situation (See Psalm 119:115.) Our children innocently enough do not grasp the tremendous power of the spiritual warfare in the lives of the obedient. In their spiritual immaturity, they think the mere presence of godliness can radically inaugurate change in others. Consequently, they need constant reminders of God's warning to be cautious in such situations: "Do not be misled: Bad company corrupts good character" (1 Corinthians 15:33). God is always right. Eventually, most become like those with whom they surround themselves.

Though I advise my children to remove themselves from ungodly influences in their lives and those who simply have no moral regard for the choices they make, I also emphasize that they should love and pray for such people from afar because prayer is undoubtedly the sole powerful, effective way to bring about change—though such change must be invited by the individual who becomes aware that change is necessary. Our continued prayer is ever before Jesus moving Him to draw the individual to Him (See John 6:44.) As the Holy Spirit convicts the world (unbelievers) of sin and as the Father draws the individual, the individual can then choose to seize the opportunity to become a believer (See John 16:8.)

I make this suggestion to my children as a result of my very own experience. Some years ago, when I lived my life merely as a professed Christian, I made the decision to no longer affiliate myself with a certain individual. Though my reasons for disassociating myself with this person were not scripturally based then, my choice saved both my marriage and me.

The decision made in this particular situation did not require scriptural justification. It did not require Christianity. It only required simple common sense. I understood, as we all do, the severity of the impact on the lives of others caused by those whose goal it is to consistently degrade people. It is always wise, if able, to remove ourselves from this lethal environment. And this is exactly what I chose to do.

In the presence of this person, without fail, controlling and manipulative words were launched at me. I began to wonder if this individual was even aware of the deadly words they incessantly spoke. Was it possible that such speech was commonplace for this individual in that it was hurled at everyone or was this degradation only hurled at me?

In the beginning, my mind valiantly fought off such contemptible words. I knew I was not that person described as such, but in time I began to believe the words uttered. I

Vile

illogically reasoned that there must be truth to what was said since malevolent words were hurled continuously. I lived, *if you hear it long enough, you begin to believe it.* And once we begin to believe something, those words manifest themselves in us—we become the ruinous words spoken with pure rancor. Because those words corrupted my character, my character in turn, corrupted the lives of those around me.

I often thought, *Today will be the day that I confront and stifle this individual who speaks such evil words.* But because my husband requested I not rock the boat thus causing unnecessary waves, I never followed through out of respect for him. But in doing so, I slowly began to resent him. I knew his petition was to prevent confrontation, spare hurt feelings and avoid a possible lifelong regret. However, I began to question if somewhere in his heart, he inconspicuously agreed with the words being said about me.

As the years passed, the words never stopped and our marriage was suffering because my resentment towards my husband was ever increasing. This resentment grew each time we saw this person. As our children got older, our visits became less frequent but not the criticizing words, nor the feelings I carried towards my husband.

When I finally decided I could no longer allow the mistreatment directed at me, I simply stopped having, altogether, any affiliation with this individual. It was my hope that in withdrawing myself from such an environment, my mind would begin to regenerate. Unfortunately, we are in some way, good or bad, a product of our environment—this is inevitable. But, in removing ourselves from such company, we create for ourselves an opportunity to be renewed. With unremitting effort this regeneration then becomes an inevitable, conspicuous growth resulting only from the long-awaited stifling of the enemy. The enemy knows no restrictions in his delivered destruction. He uses whomever and whatever to successfully achieve annihilation of God's people. But when God's people rise up against the enemy's tactics in the power of the Holy Spirit, we stifle the enemy's progress.

I realized after many years that I was the target of such discriminatory words because I was perceived as a threat. Looking back now, and certainly not then, I am saddened to think that there are individuals who, in the absence of their own self-esteem and confidence, attempt to look and feel superior by making others feel inferior. My sadness is the result of spiritual maturity. When we permit Him to do so, the Spirit is quite adept at converting our once-harbored anger and contempt for someone into peace and sympathy for that someone. These newfound feelings of peace and sympathy birth a desire within to readily eject feelings of bitterness that distance us from Jesus.

Vile

As Christians, we would never admittedly claim that sometimes the choices made by men of perverse heart influence the choices we, as Christians, make. We attempt to powerfully assert our independence by declaring that in no way do we conform to the lifestyle choices of others. We realize that our flesh is weak and our will possesses the power to dominate as the heart's desire to fulfill its lustful attraction prevails. It is then that we silently admit God's directive to steer clear of men of perverse heart, has proven itself.

At some point, we acknowledge God's precepts as evidence of His dying love for us and not His desire to make our lives miserable. We only and always benefit greatly from His guidance. And with *His* guidance, we can potentially avoid many of life's regrets.

I Choose God

I will have nothing to do with evil. – Psalm 101:4

God's guidance is not suggestion (See Psalm 119:4.) Every line is a proven declaration that should motivate us to remain within the confines of obedience. In having nothing to do with evil, we are not to partake of it nor are we to commit it. Though the Scripture is one line, it comes with two responsibilities. We must adhere to both to prevent finding ourselves in a precarious predicament.

At a previous place of employment, a few coworkers decided to start a book club. I had enjoyed participating in such a club some years previously. This wonderful pastime promoted much socialization and eating and not so much book discussion.

I expressed interest in attending in hopes that this book club would be much like the previous one. An email to employees was generated and sent out containing the name and price of the book. I contemplated making the first purchase as it was considered a must-read book. I hadn't heard of the book title, so I asked around to find out about the general story line. A fellow employee ranted and raved about how good this highly recommended book was supposed to be based on both the reviews she had read and those received from friends. She told me she'd email me a synopsis of the book. Once I received it and read it, I thought to myself, *There's no way I can read this book.*

As I headed home that night after work, I began to think to myself that maybe I was overreacting a bit. Maybe just *reading* it wouldn't be offensive to God. The *maybe* should have been the first and only confirmatory clue I needed to conclude that it most certainly would be offensive and that I most certainly would be partaking of evil.

Initially after reading the book synopsis, I unquestionably knew I was to decline the invitation to participate.

Vile

But I still tried to justify attending merely to enjoy the socializing and food. I reasoned, *I'll just read this one book, attend the book club get-together and soon enough, another book will be chosen that is nothing like this one.* No sooner than I had ended that sentence did I hear the Spirit speak, *it is pornography whether you see it or read it.* Undoubtedly, I needed to reject the invite, but I just didn't know how to renege on my initial invite. I didn't want to share with them why I had changed my mind. As unsaved people, the group wouldn't understand my spiritual reasoning for the change of heart. I decided not to make this decision so difficult. In the end, I just emailed everyone to say I was not interested in participating. No questions were asked and it was done.

All evil causes us to digress. It destroys our obedient walk with Christ. The disobedience is the evil we've permitted to infiltrate our minds. The disobedience pushes us back two steps thus defeating each successful step forward in obedience. Ultimately, every type of evil causes significant impairment to our relationship and walk with Christ Jesus. In renovating our souls, we choose to forgo any evil that would disrupt our faithfulness and righteousness. We voluntarily choose to take no part in that which would serve only to cause misfortune, trouble and mistrust in our lives.

Fortunately, it's much easier for us to bow out of the evil that surrounds us when our leaving won't be noticed. The

Holy Spirit beckons our dismissal from the group setting where the subject content and the language that describes it are offensive at best. In these times, we *can* walk away inconspicuously from the group. And we choose to do so, of course, because we will not voluntarily jeopardize our standing with Jesus. At times, there are some things we simply cannot control, but in the things that we can, we choose God.

In choosing God, we are choosing to reject evil. However, just when I think I've taken all the appropriate safeguards to shun evil from my life, another creative pathway pops up to expose it to me all over again. Our enemy, the devil, is chock-full of inventive ways to subject us to evil.

Before I began writing this book, my nightly routine consisted of unwinding from the stresses of the day in front of a television. It is quite amazing how protective God becomes over those who maintain a committed personal relationship with Him thereby striving to glorify God in all aspects of their lives. One evening while watching television, at the very first commercial break, I suddenly felt this zealous earnestness to change the channel. I am all too familiar with the Holy Spirit's promptings, but *this* particular prompting took me by surprise as I am not wholeheartedly engrossed in the commercials. I hurriedly tuned in with my eyes and mind to see if this prompting was in fact of the Holy Spirit—it most assuredly was. As I stood there watching, I realized that even the commercials include appalling and insulting vile content. And yet, this illusory tactic luring solely those consumers who find such content appealing has proven successful in consumer product purchase. I immediately understood the need to change channels. It was then that I realized that God, out of His love for me, was protecting me from evil. I intentionally chose the drama and sitcoms that I routinely watched according to the Holy Spirit's guidance, but I had honestly given little to no thought to what I was viewing in commercials and previews for other programming.

Needless to say, my chosen relaxation pastime has changed dramatically. My continued peace rests in praying, reading the Bible and writing for God. In those rare instances when I do watch television, I am acutely aware of this devious pathway for evil. I unhesitatingly turn the channel as God's protection leads me. I choose God.

Yet another creative and damaging pathway the devil uses is the radio. Not long ago, I was listening to the car radio while running errands when a song came on that I've always liked because of the tune. I hadn't heard it in quite some time but as the song progressed, I heard the Holy Spirit say, *Change the station.* I was completely taken aback. At first I thought to myself, *Did I hear that right?*

I kept listening thinking I must be mistaken because I couldn't immediately understand *why* I needed to change the radio station. As I continued listening, it was as if the instruments ceased and the words alone were all I could hear as they were penetrating my mind. I knew then, as I hear once again, *change the station* exactly *why* I needed to switch stations.

It is imperative to always try to understand the *why* of God's request. The teachable moment in *understanding* the why provides lifelong wisdom that secures our competency in discerning any future promoted evil. We can then make the choice to avoid the evil before the Holy Spirit needs to intervene.

This particular song was about a love affair—a woman who was involved with two men at one time. In her eyes, this was an acceptable way of life because it could afford her the best of both worlds, since each man could provide what the other could not. In all the times I'd heard that song, I had never before been prompted to change the radio station. This was probably because I was not taking in the words with any thought. Because I had previously lived as a professed Christian, my heart and mind were nonresponsive to the identity of anything offensive to the Lord. And because I neglected to seek a personal relationship with Jesus, I wouldn't have heard or discerned the Holy

Vile

Spirit's prompting to protect me from the evil saturating my mind. My entire thought process was not one that revolved around godly choices.

Relationships thrive on love, commitment and full disclosure. These binding attributes aren't sudden, but rather bud and bloom over time. In God's love, He longs to protect us just as He longs for our continued relationship with Him. His love forewarns us to set no vile thing before our eyes, to keep men of perverse heart far from us, and to have nothing to do with evil. We will not be corrupted. We choose God.

CHAPTER SIX

Act

*As we **Act**, we make an impact.*

I'm sure we've all experienced that lingering, hovering-above-us feeling as if someone is watching us, though we aren't certain what has caused the feeling to stir within us. We admit to ourselves as evidenced in our sigh of relief how very glad we are that though this feeling may wax and wane, it is only momentary.

But in reality, we *are* being watched. First and foremost, ceaselessly, by our Heavenly Father, (See Psalm 121:3) but we are also being watched by those around us. At all times, someone is witness to all that we do and say: be it good or bad, respectful or disrespectful, kind or unkind, positive or negative, holy or unholy. Though we do not consciously give thought to this as we approach each day, all eyes are definitely upon us. So, as we act, we make an impact.

Our Lives Speak Gratitude

Always giving thanks to God the Father for everything, in the name of our Lord Jesus Christ. – Ephesians 5:20

Circumstances and events recently unfolded in my life, so that I pleasantly had the opportunity to be a full-time homemaker. I was in a dead-end job with less-than-noticeable raises, very much underappreciated for my honesty and though I legitimately only carried one title, my duties included that of five titles. My hours at this job were being rearranged, and certainly not at my request. So, it was then that I decided to hand in my resignation. This decision was made all the easier because my husband had recently taken a position where the opportunity for overtime was substantial. I give thanks to You and praise Your holy name.

My husband's job has always provided the flexibility to choose his hours, permitting one of us to always be home to care for our children. In all my working years, I've only worked part-time while he maintained a full-time status. At one point, early after earning my bachelor's degree, I thought I wanted a career. But with the arrival of our children, I quickly changed my mind. I longed to be home. Even when all the kids were in school, I maintained my part-time status since it fit our schedules and as long as we were able to swing this life financially, there seemed no

Act

logical reason to change what was working. I give thanks to You and praise Your holy name.

I've never thought of myself as the kind of person to take things for granted. I was most thankful for the opportunity life presented that allowed both my husband and myself to be the sole caretakers of our children. My husband and I didn't have to struggle with the attempt to find trusting care for our children. I give thanks to You and praise Your holy name.

I don't remember ever directly linking the good in the lives of my husband and me with God as the source. These accidental opportunities, those we didn't purposely create for ourselves, were understood by me as, no more or no less than, life. And sometimes life is good in such a way that an accidental opportunity presents itself whereby we are in a position to take advantage of it.

But as we begin to mature in our walk with Christ in the renovating of our souls, though we've heard of blessings and we understand God as the source of those, we can now begin to claim, to acknowledge that these accidental opportunities are, in fact, on-purpose blessings. He is the source of all good things in our lives. I give thanks to You and praise Your holy name.

It's sort of like when someone wishes another *good luck*. I used to speak that very same well wish, but I realize now that luck plays no role in anything in the life of a Christian. But in the life of an unsaved individual, good luck is everything as they do not have God working His favor in their lives. They have not the guarantee of God and His unbroken promises or vows upon which to place their hope. So, good luck is, in fact, the best the unsaved can wish for.

As saved individuals, we need no good luck. We have the Almighty King working on our behalf. He is our hope in all things and as we put our hope in Him, we trust that His favor will rest upon us. He never breaks His promises and our obedience allows us to live the blessings of His promises. We should acknowledge God as the source of all that is good, wonderful, and rich in our lives and in doing so we acknowledge the truth that God is compassionate and gracious. Every single day, sometimes in new ways and always in the same ways, I recognize the hand of God as the source by which my daily life is carried out. I give thanks to You and praise Your holy name.

In reading this precept, always giving thanks, we might initially interpret *always* as the reminder not to be neglectful in giving praise for those "out-of-the-blue," "unexpected," "arrived-sooner-than-expected," blessings. But largely in contrast to these momentary, maybe seldom praises, *always giving praise* is the response to our intentional recognition of God's part in every aspect of our daily lives.

Act

As I set out to live always giving thanks to God for everything, it seemed only logical to begin where I see Him the most, outdoors. As an avid walker, I take in the flowering bushes and trees while simultaneously inhaling their sweet fragrance. I thank God. I hear the birds chirping and I praise God.

In our praise, we begin to notice the intricacy of God only as the Holy Spirit moves us into a recognition of God that we hadn't taken notice of initially. For example, in the praise for the flowers, I began to think about the process of photosynthesis. Though the actual process of photosynthesis isn't visible, it is no less at the hand of God. Often times, we begin our gratitude in the things that are seen, but it is quite the case that God will move us into a gratitude for the things not seen.

In my continued walk, I begin to thank Him that my joints move as they should. I thank Him for my heart that sufficiently pumps blood throughout my body. These functions take place only by the hand of God.

When I am tired, I am thankful to lay my head upon a pillow that is lying on a mattress. I cover myself with blankets that keep me warm. I am thankful for a dependable vehicle to travel in. When I climb into the driver's seat, I notice the gas gauge: it is full. I am thankful to give no thought as to whether to take my children to the doctor's office. When asked for an insurance card, I am blessed to present one.

In every part of my day, I recognize God in some way. In prayer, I often express my concern that somehow speaking the words, *I'm thankful*, doesn't adequately reflect just *how* thankful to God I really am.

My husband used to remind me, rather frequently, to accept the blessings from God without thinking they were delivered with a cost. My overwhelming guilt weighed heavily as I felt so undeserving. I felt that an exchange needed to take place: something given for the blessing received. I pictured the scales of justice having to remain balanced between myself and God.

And I furthered this warped thinking with the thought of how nice it would be if the blessings came with a receipt. I would then have the option to return some of them to get something of lesser value so as to somehow match my worth. My worth, in and of myself, so very little, magnified the appreciation of the blessings.

I have finally come to the understanding that there really are no words in the human language to adequately express my gratitude to God for the goodness of Him in my life. I realize that living my life obediently, faithfully and righteously is the one and only exchange that can suitably and appropriately declare my gratefulness. As I act, I make an impact.

Act

Our Tour Guide

Direct my footsteps according to your word; let no sin rule over me. – Psalm 119:133

As parents, we want the best for our children. In fact, as parents, we yearn for them to far exceed all that we ourselves ever accomplished. We long for them to have every opportunity to advance in both their physical lives as well as their spiritual lives. The assumption is that if they are advancing spiritually then they are advancing physically in their daily lives. As parents supplying our children with our insight and guidance, whether sought by them or not, it is hopeful that they lead lives with very little regret.

As parents of young believers, we notice that they are unlikely to engage in seeking God through His Word. Parents take great care to create a worry-free environment for their children: "remember your Creator in the days of your youth, before the days of trouble come" (See Eccl. 12:1.) Because of this, unlike adults, children are not as apt to routinely seek God whether in His Word or in prayer. This innocent gap between themselves and God is in no way reflective of their incredible reverence for Him. However, a personal relationship and knowledge of the Word of God is the only effective means to bring closure to this gap between themselves and God. And in time, as they age and mature, this will happen. Until then, as parents, *we* actually deliver God's Word to them in every teachable moment that presents itself to guide them. We do with our children just as Jeremiah did, "obey the Lord by doing what I tell you" (Jeremiah 38:20).

As prayer warriors for our children, our prayers are exclusive to our own children. For my children, I ask God that as doors are closed, He would open windows along the narrow corridors of life that my children journey. My heart yearns for them to remain on the narrow road that leads to life (See Matthew 7:14.)

Regardless of the route, closed doors are inevitable. But I ask God to allow the already closed doors to remain closed and to open a window instead, as it is effortless to cross the threshold of an already open door. As the doors remain closed, my children are forced to continue their travel along this narrow route in hopes of discovering an open window. After many closed doors, an open window is welcomed and they realize that the open window is only at the hand of God.

Because human beings are naturally inquisitive, they unhesitatingly pursue the quest to receive what God has awaiting for them. To retrieve the blessing, they are required to confront the inconvenience and difficulty of getting through the window. This struggle fosters determination,

Act

steadfastness and stamina to seize all God has for them. His love and care for them is teaching invaluable strengths that will aid my children as they continue to travel the corridors of life in search of open windows.

Just as we pray for our children, we avidly pray for guidance in our own journey. But before becoming a believer who sought God to direct our steps, our lives as an unbeliever was nothing more than our own attempt to get from point A to point B. This attempt to get from point A, the beginning of our lives, to point B, the end of our lives, was walked in darkness. We wandered aimlessly in our own effort to achieve this. As unbelievers, we would feel our way through the darkness.

But as believers, God leads us in His light. In seeking God's governance in our lives, we are inviting Him to direct our footsteps, and the knowledge of His Word is the necessary preliminary to live let no sin rule over me.

This precept isn't necessarily a directive to abandon the road we're on, but it is a directive to abandon the road if it falls outside the boundaries of God. Falling outside these established boundaries is falling into sin. And if our deepest desire is to actually live "direct my footsteps according to Your Word" then with no hesitation, whatsoever, we abandon and we bail on that which would have asked us to disregard God's Word.

Direct our footsteps is about obedience. And God is the required help to let no sin rule over us. As we trek this expedition of life, we can find security in knowing that God directs our footsteps if we allow Him to do so. But in order to discern His governance in our lives, we must possess familiarity with His Word. We render ourselves incapable of ascertaining the established boundaries of God if we are remiss in our responsibility to know God's Word. Our own effort to prevent sin from consuming our lives is a fruitless endeavor. In choosing to live within the boundaries established by His Word, we have more than willingly surrendered pursuit of our own direction and have joyfully given to Him our destiny.

Along this narrow route, God is growing and stretching us beyond our self-imposed limits. He is slowly revealing that with Him, there are no limits. This growing and stretching is vital to the fruition of His divine purpose for our lives.

There will be times we find ourselves confused as He directs our footsteps due to our own weakness in allowing our once-surrendered, self-guided direction to creep back into our lives. We cannot permit ourselves to interfere in His leading.

When a quarterback throws a pass, he hopes that his pass is successfully caught by his receiver—without a sudden interception by the opposing team. God wants the same thing from us. As He directs our footsteps, He wants no interference from us in the form of questioning, doubting and second-guessing. With God, we are either all in to win, or we are all out because we doubt. His goal for all is that we are wholeheartedly desiring to be directed in our footsteps. But this longing must be genuine or the second half of this precept, let no sin rule over me, will be useless. In the absence of sin, we are obedient. Our obedience is the gateway for the delivery of His favor. Let God grant us immunity from the enemy's vicious lure as we call on Him to preside over our direction.

Not Ours, But His

*Asking God to fill you with the knowledge of **his** will through all spiritual wisdom and understanding.* – Colossians 1:9 (author emphasis)

I was looking forward to college in hopes that it would be much different than high school. I was intimidated by the thought of going only because I didn't know what to expect. I had a fear of the unknown. While I waited for school to begin, I gave in to worry all too often: *How long will it take me to become familiar with the campus? Am I sure about the major I decided to study? What if college ends up like high school?*

I knew I'd do well academically because I had done so well in high school. The only fear I didn't have was the comfort of studying the assigned material and writing papers.

To my surprise, as I am directionally challenged, I successfully made my way to my very first college class. As class began, the professor handed out a syllabus. This was a new term for me, but one that I became grateful to know. I function well with some sort of daily itinerary or routine. I find security in knowing what each day holds. The syllabus was the unexpected gift that provided certainty for me in a new, uncertain environment.

The college syllabus served as the itinerary for the entire semester. It included test dates and final exam dates. It provided the professor's contact information, his goal for the class and included all the vital components necessary to complete a research paper—the required length, topics from which to choose, the necessary format, and the number of pages required. I loved it. What was for me a new discovery had long been instituted in colleges. What seemed so insignificant to others was a luxury to me. It allowed me to rearrange my work schedule in advance as needed so that I could complete projects, study for finals and write papers by the required deadlines.

My high school experience never afforded me the itinerary benefit. Sure, I routinely attended the same classes all year with the same teachers and students, but I was never given in advance, quiz and test dates and whether a research paper would be required for the class. At the teacher's discretion, test dates were suddenly scheduled which permitted only a couple days of study time to prepare. And when a teacher felt it necessary to drive home a concept, suddenly a research paper was assigned in order to accomplish that goal.

As an education major, I learned that teachers are required to meet state-mandated standards for each subject. For me, state standards were yet another incredible concept since these standards, like a syllabus, also served as an itinerary or guideline from which to work. My high school teachers had a syllabus already written for them by the state. I often wondered why they just didn't modify this state syllabus by simply adding due dates alongside each required standard then handing them out in class at the beginning of the school year, thereby making life so much easier for students.

As students working to become teachers, we referenced these standards every day. It was crucial that our lesson plans incorporated them to be certain we had achieved completion of that state standard. The college syllabus and state standard guidelines were expected to be followed to efficaciously fulfill the requirements of those who created them. They were not my requirements. I was just expected to know them and implement them.

Just as I never questioned the state standards and syllabus requirements, I do not question God's divine plan for my life—just the opposite, I long to know it that I may intentionally step into it. It would be rather difficult to know God's purpose for our lives if we were never in the process of asking Him to fill us with the knowledge of *His* will.

In general, all practicing Christians share overlapping responsibilities in living God's will. Examples include living our lives "for the praise of his glory" (Ephesians 1:12) and "to give his people the knowledge of salvation through the forgiveness of sins" (Luke 1:77). However, in asking God to fill us with the knowledge of His will for our own life, it then becomes personal. And God has a specific will that is exclusive to the life of each individual.

For some, in seeking God's will for their lives, there is an expectation that if it is not grand and visible for all to see, then His will for them is not worth their effort. What we fail to understand is that every single purpose for every single person *is* grand and *is* visible. By default, it is grand because we are fulfilling the purpose expressed by royalty—the King of kings and it is seen because as we are fulfilling God's purpose, we are exuding the character of Christ.

Every job that each person maintains in the production of a Broadway play or even a movie is incredibly

Act

significant—from those who are in charge of lighting, costumes and set creation, to the writers, performers and those who choreograph the music. Neither play nor movie goes off without a hitch unless each and every person does his job efficaciously.

God has the same plan to further His kingdom. We each play a most invaluable role in leading others to salvation, living lives that leave others thirsting for what we have, maintaining our exemplary emulation of Christ Jesus in our daily living, and stepping into our very own unique purpose according to God's will. Without the notable work of *every* Christian, each specific role filled only by a specific person, according to the will of God, would considerably slow the advancement of God's kingdom. The focus of our godly jobs is not visibility and grandness, for these are only temporary. The focus of each role is eternity, upon which no monetary value can be placed.

Obviously, God's will for our lives, also the essential foundation of every Christian life, is to continuously familiarize ourselves with His syllabus (His Word), which outlines *His* standards by which we are to abide (See Psalm 119:4.) However, God's syllabus is void of due dates because the *entirety* of our lives is familiarizing ourselves with His Word and living His standards. Gaining knowledge of the spiritual wisdom found in God's Word and then applying the understanding of it in how we actually live is God's will for every Christian's life. If we cannot, first, live God's general will for all Christians, then we inflict upon ourselves a severe handicap by rendering ourselves utterly incapable of living God's specific will for us as individuals.

God's syllabus (His Word) is not an elective teaching, rather it is the required course of study that provides us a necessary spiritual wisdom. There is no mention of pop quizzes, unexpected exams, and research papers in His syllabus as we should be daily living the teaching provided. As we seek God to fill us with the knowledge of His will and as we dedicate ourselves to faithfully walk in the revealed will for our lives, we fulfill all syllabus requirements.

Our Heart's Desire

Whatever you do, work at it with all your heart, as working for the Lord, not for men. It is the Lord Christ you are serving.
– Colossians 3:23, 24

I give one hundred percent in everything I do—why put forth the effort if I'm going to give any less than my best. Though I gave a hundred percent in my previous job, my periodic performance reviews inaccurately reflected the opposite. I could never quite achieve the numbers needed to move me into the highest tier, which would have allowed for the maximum raise. I longed to be in the highest tier not for the raise, but because *that* tier would have accurately reflected my effort in bringing resolution to every problem.

I worked in a call center whose primary focus was to clear waiting calls without any regard, and I mean *any* regard, to much-needed resolution to customer problems. And any customer service agent who met the production requirement in number of calls taken per hour, regardless of how the agent made that happen, was rewarded. Often, a caller would end up on my line after having *just* spoken to another representative who did not grant the service the caller was entitled to—problem resolution. In fact, most of the other agents transferred calls, without warrant, in order to satisfy the production requirement that successfully landed them in the highest tier, thereby affording them the opportunity to receive the maximum raise.

For me, it was most inhumane to rush the caller along or to conveniently transfer a call simply to benefit *me* so that I could meet a production requirement. I put myself in that caller's predicament every single time. I cannot count the number of times *I* have been in that very same situation, transferred numerous times, pawned onto someone else only to find out I had been in the right place to begin with.

As we genuinely and wholeheartedly live Colossians 3:23, our entire persona is radically reformed. We do the very same tasks and then some, but our mentality and intention to the completion of them is wondrously new. We have a newfound pleasure in knowing, in all that we do, *He* is pleased with the repaired motive that drives us to tackle our daily commitments.

I take the *whatever you do* portion of this Scripture literally. I do things now that I wouldn't have chosen to do otherwise, knowing it is done for Christ. For example, I will stop to pick up boxes of food that lie in the grocery store aisles and restore them to their shelf. As consumers rummage through department store clothing, clothes naturally fall from hangers and shelves. I don't walk around the clothing to avoid it. I gather the clothes and place them on a nearby shelf to prevent them from being destroyed. On windy trash collection days, inevitably, trash cans make their way into the street. When I pull into my subdivision and see a trash can blowing around in the middle of the neighborhood street, I pull over and move the can back to the sidewalk.

Before the discovery of this Scripture, we did not consider how a once seemingly insignificant *act* suddenly becomes a most meaningful *role* as everything we do, we do it for Christ. In working for Him, we never have to prepare a magnificent resume or conduct a flawless interview. We inherited this most worthwhile service when we became

Act

children of God—and we landed job security, something the secular world cannot offer. We forever maintain our position in serving Christ. In the Kingdom world, this position is permanent.

Furthermore, our performance evaluation administered by Jesus is not based on production numbers that point out an employee's incompetence. Nor are we subjected to the skewed opinions of man since Jesus evaluates our performance. Our evaluation by Him is based solely on the motives of our heart. We no longer failingly search for man's approval, as the only approval we long to gain is that of Jesus. In hearing Christ speak, *with him I am well pleased*, (See Matt. 3:17) we know we have successfully accomplished the only approval that matters most to us—the approval of Christ.

As Christians, we should more so operate with a keen attitude and clear conscience, in honesty without sin, in whatever capacity we function, whether it be a pharmaceutical representative, a car salesman, a waiter or a teacher. Initially, our motive for performing these duties to the very best of our ability may have been solely for financial advancement. However, in whatever capacity we serve as Christians, our *primary* incentive should not be material gain, which is temporal, but eternal gain. If we've ever struggled in giving our best, for whatever reason, it is hopeful that we will struggle no more, as our newest heart's desire is to do all things as though working for the Lord and not for men. When we live this, we automatically do all that we do with a greater awareness of the needs of others thus fulfilling both our spiritual and physical roles.

CHAPTER SEVEN

Train

Train that we might remain.

If we could seize the excitement that children possess in learning and remain in the mindset of a child—where the wonder of everything new is met with awe and learning is a welcomed adventure waiting to unfold—our lives would be much fuller of wisdom and knowledge. But more often than not, learning is not a welcomed endeavor for most as we have become set in our ways. Instead, our tolerated learning is the means by which we achieve a tangible end.

For example, a new job requires much to be learned. The training classes seem long and never ending, and we understand very little until we actually begin to perform the job. But we push through knowing that the job is a means to a very necessary end—a paycheck.

Unfortunately, as we age, we get set in our ways and our daily itinerary. Learning new things seems laborious and time consuming, especially if what is being taught necessitates stepping out of the comfortable routine we've led for so long. And if learning new *things* seems laborious and time consuming, what about learning to become a brand-new person? And comfort zone—there is none when learning to institute a set of Bible-based standards for a new type of daily living that inevitably reconstructs who we once were.

Knowledge Is Not Automatic

Teach me knowledge and good judgment. – Psalm 119:66

All that I know, I have been taught. This isn't to say that all I've been taught is all that I choose to be. I acknowledge that some of what's been taught is bad, most things good, but still, all things taught. I never understood that this *teaching me knowledge and good judgment* was something I would have needed so badly. I longed to be someone different and, in this longing, I knew something would be required of me—having the *desire* for God to teach me *His* knowledge and *His* good judgment. In order to implement God's knowledge and judgment in my life, I would need to forgo quite a bit of my own knowledge. The same goes for my own judgment as well. This I welcomed because it was apparent that my way of doing things was just not working.

I was living a life of discouragement and disharmony. The peace and order I desired seemed only an imaginary end result. Only after I had exhausted all *my* ways of resolving issues and only after I was fed up with being fed up did I finally recognize the only life-saving answer was Jesus Himself. This is why I began to pursue Him as I did. I was all too familiar with sin as I was drenched in it. Changing on my own had proven unsuccessful, to say the least. And I was fearful that this much-required change, once implemented, would not last.

God's entire Word is a lesson waiting to be taught to a willing student and I was willing at that point in my life . . . willing to step out of my comfort zone, longing to gain godly knowledge and godly judgment that I may engage in choices that were representative of my salvation. I reasoned that these choices would have to produce a life of the peace and order I longed for. Choices that would grow a new me, thereby growing a new life—one that was not in any way reflective of the life I was currently leading. Choices that upon self-reflection would reveal a Christlike character, something I'd not ever intentionally given thought to.

I wanted to change, and I wanted this change to be permanent. I was tired of living life as the person I was and, as *life* isn't changeable, *I* had to be. In my life, some days were good, some days were spent in the valley, most days lived just going through the motions, but all those days were lived without Christ. I longed to be led on level ground (See Psalm 143:10.)

Unfortunately, no one just automatically knows how to live obediently in this newly saved life. Once saved, the Lord longs to teach us. Our part in His plan is to *desire* this teaching and to seek Him for it. Contrary to my own popular persuasion, this knowledge isn't somehow involuntarily imparted to us the moment we are saved.

I lived this preconceived notion—as a Christian, I would automatically be transformed. As I got older and the events of my life unfolded, I was changing, oh boy was I changing, but I certainly did not like the person I was becoming. And if I didn't like the person I was, how much more disappointed was God? I finally realized I needed a major renovation in my life—a soul renovation—and I knew that the only way this would happen was if I asked Christ daily to teach me knowledge and good judgment. This request of Christ required my full commitment if this was to become my chosen lifestyle.

I feared repeating my past track record by choosing to seek God only intermittently. In making this unwise choice, I forced large gaps of time without Him thus severely delaying the affirmation that change was necessary. I was all too familiar with these gaps. I didn't begin to attend church until I was married, and church was exciting at first. Though the environment was unfamiliar to me, I felt no fear in this unfamiliarity. Everything was new and filled me with awe. I felt incredible joy and peace. I loved the singing and the people, but I especially awaited the sermon with great anticipation—I loved the teaching. I temporarily possessed the mindset of a child where everything new is met with awe.

I wanted this newness to remain with me always. I prayed. I read. I studied. But at some point, the more I read, the more discouraged I became. First, I found the Word very difficult to understand. Second, based on what I did understand, I convinced myself I would never be able to live my life like Christ. Third, it became increasingly more difficult to pray because I felt so discouraged. Little by little, I slipped away from all of it. I stopped reading, praying and going to church. I found excuses for the choices I made, and these excuses gave me peace. But in the cessation of it all, I was losing all that I had gained with the Father—the beginning of a personal relationship and the peace I lived as a result.

I wish I had realized then that had I just kept plowing through, I would have discovered that in God's incredible love for me, He had already provided a teacher. This teacher, His Holy Spirit, abides with me forever that I might no longer feel discouraged in my attempt to understand the Word of God. "But the Counselor, the Holy Spirit, whom the Father will send in my name, will teach you all things and will remind you of everything I have said to you" (John 14:26).

God understands the undisputable magnitude of the importance of teaching. Even His Son was taught by Him. *Jesus gave them this answer: "I tell you the truth, the Son can do nothing by himself; he can do only what he sees his Father doing, because whatever the Father does the Son also does. For the Father loves the Son and shows him all he does"* (John 5:19-20). The spiritual growth that results from the lessons taught is of such incredible importance that His own Son does all things as His Father teaches Him. I, too, yearned for My Father's teaching. The Holy Spirit's revelation of the meaning of the precept is the comprehension needed to efficaciously apply the lesson to our lives. Without the understanding, the concept is simply forgotten and because it is forgotten, a most valuable precept to aid in daily living falls by the wayside when it could have been the very Word needed to serve as our lifeline. His lessons are the building materials needed to grow godliness. This good and godly teaching is the fundamental prerequisite needed to practice good and godly judgment.

This teaching is a progression. I long for it daily. As Jesus was taught by His Father, the disciples were taught by Jesus, and as all Scripture is God-breathed (See 2nd Timothy 3:16), we are taught the Scriptural truths by the Holy Spirit. I am no longer discouraged. I have hope that comprehension will ultimately be unveiled by the Holy Spirit. I trust that, in God's time, I will understand.

Knowledge is Power

Knowledge is power is an understood concept by both the saved and the unsaved. However, God-knowledge is *more* power because it is the manual for daily living (See 2 Peter 1:3), the roadmap needed for journeys, and the prescribed medicine for all the headaches that accompany both. All this knowledge is offered in a free, all-inclusive "handbook" that empowers *me* for daily living. I can face each and every day with power, armed with a godly knowledge to assist me in every emotional aspect of my life because, for the most part, most problems stem from emotional issues.

Societal knowledge, on the other hand, is not offered in a free, all-inclusive handbook that actually empowers one with the knowledge needed to thrive in all aspects of daily living. Society teaches to pursue one kind of knowledge because society usually associates knowledge with some type of schooling. So, for example, as one contemplates his career, society suggests to choose a field, particularly one that is of interest and pursue an education in that subject. The more knowledge one gains in a particular field, as they are specializing in that field, society deems one an "expert." And most often, people seek professional help from experts who specialize in an individual's area of interest.

For example, let's say a couple is having marital issues they're unable to rectify on their own, so they decide to seek a marriage counselor. Obviously, counselors can specialize in the field of marriage. *"These therapists have graduate or postgraduate degrees—and many choose to become credentialed by the American Association for Marriage and Family Therapy (AAMFT)."*[2] In seeking expert guidance, society thrives on the concept of an "all-knowing" individual. Couples find solace in the purported promise of such counselors to bring resolution to a conflicted marriage. These experts testify to their surefire methods for repairing marital relationships.

Discernibly, marital problems necessitate countless visits before the issues are resolved, and at that, resolution is never guaranteed. Countless couples throw in the towel because they've either run out of money, met the maximum allowable visits approved by their insurance company, stop attending the sessions because life requires them to be other places that they feel are of greater importance, or they've simply lost all hope and don't know how to get it back.

Train

But God's Word, full of knowledge, is *more* powerful than any knowledge society has to offer (See 1 Corinthians 3:19.) The free Counselor in His free book can restore lost hope, provide the necessary life-guiding precepts (See 2 Peter 1:3) and equip the couple seeking help with the power needed (the Holy Spirit) to implement the guiding principles that bring resolution.

I am learning that the starting point, the very commencement of allowing God to bring resolution to the issues in my life by *His* counsel, regardless of what those issues might be, consists of two extremely vital qualities: possessing the love of Christ and prayer.

Possessing the love with which God loves His creation inspires us to forgive and something good and full of love is bound to result from forgiveness—always. Most often the act of forgiveness is the dawning of resolution to most problems. Secondly, prayer serves a threefold purpose. First, it invites God into our problem. Second, prayer acknowledges that we need God's help in the form of guidance and power in this relationship. Third, devout prayer changes the heart of men, and *no* human counselor with any number of specialized degrees can do this. With God, there is always hope in resolving issues.

Though I did not seek marital counseling, my marriage issues were of grave concern for me at one point in my life.

Had I actually been reading the Word of God, thereby familiarizing myself with Scripture, I could have saved my husband and myself so much torment, struggle and grief in our marriage. God knows that every marriage, I mean no marriage excluded, requires much perseverance, prayer, power of the Holy Spirit and a plethora of Scripture knowledge.

Had I been a fixed prayer and a fixed reader of God's Word, these are just a few, a *very* few, examples of Scripture I could have prayed daily, and as often as I needed to throughout the course of the day that would have jumpstarted marital repair. Undoubtedly, praying God's Word would have begun to change my heart as well as my husband's. And when hearts are hard, only the love of God can make them pliable.

> *Forgive as the Lord forgave you.*
> —Colossians 3:13
>
> *Set a guard over my mouth, O Lord; keep watch over the door of my lips.*
> —Psalm 141:3
>
> *Be imitators of God, therefore, as dearly loved children and live a life of love, just as Christ loved us.*
> —Ephesians 5:1-2
>
> *Husbands, love your wives, just as Christ loved the church and gave himself up for her.*
> —Ephesians 5:25

Train

> *Wives, submit to your husbands, as is fitting in the Lord.*
>
> —Colossians 3:18
>
> *Husbands, love your wives and do not be harsh with them.*
>
> —Colossians 3:19
>
> *Husbands, in the same way be considerate as you live with your wives, and treat them with respect as the weaker partner and as heirs with you of the gracious gift of life, so that nothing will hinder your prayers.*
>
> —1 Peter 3:7

Additionally, praying His Word can do so much in resolving issues with feelings like discouragement, fear and sorrow.

> *The righteous man is rescued from trouble…*
>
> —Proverbs 11:8
>
> *Peace I leave with you; my peace I give you. I do not give to you as the world gives. Do not let your hearts be troubled and do not be afraid.*
>
> —John 14:27
>
> *My soul is weary with sorrow; strengthen me according to your word.*
>
> —Psalm 119:28

> *When I said, "My foot is slipping," your love, O Lord, supported me. When anxiety was great within me, your consolation brought joy to my soul.*
>
> —Psalm 94:18-19

In those times when we simply cannot achieve, even after much prayer, the desired result for whatever the issue at hand may be, God still provides help in the form of professional physicians. However, it is still of such momentous importance to remain in prayer and God's Word even when seeking the help of professionals—that we may not be led astray, and because at any moment, great healing can come in whatever form needed.

Knowledge Always Precedes Good Judgment

Knowledge always precedes good judgment, or at least it should. We make judgment calls every single day, whether or not we consciously realize it. They include such decisions as whether or not to go jogging outdoors because it looks like it may rain or whether there will be enough time to stop at the grocery store before picking up the kids at school.

Judgment calls rank on a scale that includes everything from weighty issues to "just-to-keep-the-peace" judgment calls. As a mom, my judgment calls are most often those

Train

made to keep the peace so they tend to rank on the less weighty end of the scale. The judgment calls made resulted in a headache-free day for me and one in which everyone can *usually* enjoy the outcome.

I did this much more frequently when my children were younger. My judgment calls then included making trivial decisions such as who got the toy back without knowing who had it first or who would get to ride shotgun even when I couldn't remember who rode shotgun the last time we left the house.

In making a *good* judgment call regarding my children, I had to rely on my knowledge of them. Before my judgment call was rendered, I always took into account the temperament of each child, the likes and dislikes of each, and which one was more willing to go along with the program. These considerations did not result in unfair or biased treatment.

While most of my judgment calls as a young mom were not of great concern, I do recall one particular decision that *was* of great concern to me at the time. When we introduced table food to my youngest daughter, she simply didn't like anything. I remember it worried me for weeks. Getting her to eat regular food was like pulling teeth. So, I decided to keep feeding her the baby food I knew she already liked and continued trying to reintroduce regular food periodically.

Through much trial and error, we discovered the only two foods she would eat—plain mashed potatoes and yogurt. As she began to enjoy the mashed potatoes and yogurt, she slowly began rejecting the baby food. I was hopeful that as we continued to introduce more and more table food into her diet, she would eventually acquire a taste for a variety of foods. This was not the case, however, and I became understandably concerned. My agonizing thought was that there was no way mashed potatoes, yogurt, whole milk and juice could provide all the necessary nutrients she needed to progress in her development as she should. I decided to consult with her pediatrician because *I* did not possess the preceding knowledge needed to practice good judgment and I could not move forward without such knowledge. The pediatrician assured and reassured me that such eating habits were normal and that my daughter would continue to normally progress in her development. She further explained that some children are just very picky eaters and recommended that I continue to introduce new foods into her diet.

Although a physician with many years of both knowledge and experience reassured me all would be well, I was the one responsible for rendering good judgment. I had to decide whether to heed the advice of my knowledgeable pediatrician, seek a second opinion or maybe even attempt to supplement my daughter's nutrition in an alternative way. About this, I was already in prayer asking God that comfort would be the confirmation needed that in my final decision good judgment was indeed practiced. He reminded me that the matter at hand could have been so much worse. She could have rejected all table foods and stubbornly remained on baby food or she could have possibly lost her appetite altogether. I was blessed that she enjoyed the two foods that she did. I finally decided to follow my pediatrician's recommendations, and for many, many months my daughter continued to eat only plain mashed potatoes and yogurt.

Practice Doesn't Make Perfect, It Makes Obedience

Everyone is familiar with the adage, *practice makes perfect*. It's just I do not agree with it. The idea behind this adage is that the forced repetition of the action produces a flawless performance. However, the practice of something doesn't produce perfection. Instead, it highlights our imperfection. We are now—more than ever, aware of the variables, both controlled and uncontrolled, which prove that we as humans will never possess perfection. Well, at least not here on Earth.

There is no doubt that both the believer and the unbeliever agree that the word *judgment* carries a negative connotation. Believers, however, who find themselves on the receiving end of this unwelcome judgment sometimes feel falsely and unjustly accused. Their retaliation to such judgment is all too often based on an *opinion* rather than a grasped, understood and lived knowledge of the Word of God. As stated before, knowledge should always precede good judgment, but equally important is the knowledge needed to refute accusations.

In our pursuit of the acquisition of knowledge, we soon realize just how multi-faceted the word *judgment* really is in a scriptural sense. God's Word is not accurately, at times, interpreted when based on our standard dictionary definition, rather accuracy can depend on either, or possibly both, the Hebrew or the Greek interpretation of the word. *According to **Vine's Complete Expository Dictionary of Old and New Testament Words**, Thomas Nelson, 1980, **judgment** can be "perception, discernment" (p. 337), while **good** is "morally honorable and pleasing to God" (p. 273).* Good judgment is not made based on mere opinion. We accomplish our goal to render good judgment that leads to all that is morally honorable and pleasing to God by having immersed ourselves in His Word, thereby learning His precepts and obediently living them.

When asking God to teach us good judgment, we lean entirely upon our knowledge of His Word and guidance

Train

of the Holy Spirit. This is the only way that we can know *how* to live morally honorable and pleasing lives to God. Even Paul longed for the Christian people to gain more and more knowledge. "And this is my prayer: that your love may abound more and more in knowledge and depth of insight, so that you may be able to discern what is best and may be pure and blameless until the day of Christ." (Philippians 1:9).

To effectively apply *God's* good judgment, we submit ourselves entirely to His authority and guidance, but our opinions must play no role in exercising this judgment. In understanding that our opinions are facts reshaped to suit our *own* needs, it becomes apparent that our opinions would only serve to interfere with God's teaching. We only interject our opinions in an effort to maintain *our* satisfied needs. Most often, our opinions emerge because we feel His precepts disrupt our current lifestyle or we are simply not happy with what God's Word requires of us. In these times, we must recall that His goal is now our goal—to emulate Jesus. The only successful means by which this can happen is to learn as much about Him as we can through His Word. As we forge ahead in our faithfulness to execute daily God's good judgment, these initial feelings of opposition will begin to happily subside.

When we begin to institute His Word into our lives, it feels awkward and foreign only in that it is new. But the newness of His Word and the closeness we feel to Him is unmatchable. At first, we stumble. The practice makes perfect motto certainly *does* highlight our imperfections as human beings. In further familiarity with His Word, accompanied by much prayer, we practice obedience, we fall, we practice obedience, we fall, and we practice obedience. Eventually, we live it, sometimes we fall, but still, we daily practice obedience. And we long to live more and more of it.

As we delve into His precepts, we are awakened to spiritual concepts that we would not have otherwise identified as such: gossip, laziness, envy, slander and greed . . .all defects we are guilty of having initiated or taken part in at some point in our lives. We learn quickly that these are reprehensible to God.

Our earthly judgments *seem* to be the easiest to make, though at times we do not consider that they can be detrimental to both ourselves and those around us. In making a judgment call, a seed can be instantaneously planted, but sometimes we are not conscious of the fact that we even planted a seed. What we practice are the seeds we plant. If detrimental judgment calls are repeatedly made then we just planted a not-so-good seed. And a not-so-good seed yields a not-so-good harvest.

In making earthly judgment calls, we are led by a moral gauge—a gauge that differentiates between right and wrong

Train

... a gauge that seems to be broken at times as it fluctuates from person to person because we each define right and wrong differently. Some have a conscience that doesn't permit them to wander far from the *right* side of the gauge, while others are not as easily guilty, leaning more towards the *wrong* side of the gauge.

The spiritual gauge is never broken. It is incapable of fluctuating from person to person as *God* is the One who defines right from wrong, spiritual from secular, and divine from evil. He does not expect more or less from different people. He expects the same from everyone.

At times, we wrestle more with making good, spiritual judgment decisions as opposed to earthly ones. We wrestle not because we are unable to discern that which is morally honorable and pleasing to God. At times, we wrestle with good, spiritual judgment as it requires us to be spiritual in the area we are attempting to make a good judgment. And if we are not practicing that spiritual precept, a change in ourselves or our lifestyle should probably ensue. Because change is uninviting, demanding and lengthy, we sometimes choose not to practice good, spiritual judgment. In doing so, we plant the very same seed we planted in our earthly judgment. If we had stuck to our guns in our decision to go all for God or nothing, we would unquestionably sow good seeds as we chose to abide in God's precepts. And who doesn't want to reap the harvest of good seed: when we sow into the Kingdom of God, we sow the certainty of promise.

If we fail to surrender to God's authority and His precepts, we can exclude ourselves from the good that God has to offer. Nothing, absolutely nothing worth having is effortless. As a matter of fact, just the opposite is true. It is our diligent effort, devoted time and determined resolve that give worth to what's worth having. And God recognizes the effort, the time and the resolve we put forth into becoming more like Him in our thoughts and character.

God's Word has no gray areas. It is colored in only black and white: the don'ts and the do's. We choose to live it wholeheartedly, trusting the Holy Spirit's power to aid us or we choose to live only bits and pieces of it. In choosing to do the latter, we subject ourselves to the possibility of not being the heir to *all* of God's promises.

If our final decision is to live wholeheartedly for God, we have made the godly choice. We are empowered in this choice by knowing He has already made us bold and stouthearted (See Psalm 138:3.) These are not attributes that progressively grow and take shape as a result of trials and dilemmas. As His word states, "you made me bold and stouthearted" (Psalm 138:3). We already possess these attributes as a believer: received once we accepted Jesus as our Lord and Savior. He has given us the boldness to live *differently* than the unbeliever and the stoutheartedness to *live* the change in our lives. We just need to possess the will to employ the renovating power of the Spirit.

As we become conversant with His Word, we prepare ourselves to make good, spiritual judgment. This judgment is neither popular nor widely accepted as the norm. Some view Christians as odd people for whom life is quite mundane. Others *secretly* long for the life we lead. We know that practice doesn't make perfect rather practice makes obedience. We can live obedience, but as we are human, we can never live perfection. Well… at least not here on Earth.

Title Responsibilities

*Teach me to do **your** will.* – Psalm 143:10 (author emphasis)

Every title we assume, knowingly or unknowingly, is accompanied by title responsibilities. While the title is not always indicative of how menial or even how noble the duties performed may be, effort is always required to carry out those responsibilities, as each one lived efficaciously brings God the Father great glory.

Though most ordinarily we associate titles with salary, they are not limited to a professional work environment. Not all titles earn salaries, however, these titles must not be interpreted as any less significant. Sometimes, the "salary-less" titles earn so much more for us than a monetary reimbursement for our efforts.

As everything we do involves others, we carry a title—though we do not consciously acknowledge or even consider the day-to-day, ordinary, overlooked titles that we own and to which we are held accountable in our everyday lives. One such title, not usually perceived as such, is our name. Though our name is not routinely or even technically defined as a title in that it does not identify specific job duties, it is nonetheless a title that is accompanied by responsibilities. Our name bears the choices we make, identifies what we stand for and reflects whom we serve. Our name has the potential power to be either our virtue or our depravity. In our devotion to uphold a title, we must also possess the willingness to fulfill the responsibilities that accompany these meaningful titles.

Teachable

As we engage in such official titles like nurse, firefighter or C.E.O., we don't routinely give thought to the commonplace titles we currently maintain. We do not recognize that in our everyday responsibilities, we incur any number of ordinary and sometimes unacknowledged titles: mom and dad, friend and neighbor, homeowner and auto owner, landscaper and window washer. And of course, through salvation, we are privileged to gain the honorary title of Christian.

Titles mandate that we possess the distinct quality of being teachable though we don't consider this a prerequisite to the possession of the title. As teachable people, we willingly set aside any obstructive or incompatible prior thoughts or actions that have become embedded into our brain and instead humbly open our mind, heart and will to that of *Christ's* mind, heart and will. As new and teachable creatures in Christ, we are prepping ourselves to carry out the expectations of our newly-claimed title of Christian.

In setting aside our old ways and thought processes, we are not tossing them out completely—at least, not yet. We need to examine what we once practiced as an unbeliever. As even our thought processes will evolve spiritually, we engage this heightened spiritual acumen to discern those preexisting molds of ourselves that do not align with God's Word. As we identify such parts of ourselves, we toss them and replace them with godly alternatives. This desired process of elimination reveals our teachable capacity.

How Is God Like a Hiring Manager?

Our teachable capacity is an indispensable asset in every aspect of our lives. As we long to be forgiven, we demonstrate our willingness to admit our sin. And as we long to do God's will, we demonstrate our willingness to humbly exchange our will for His.

It is apparent that our willingness is the common denominator between admitting our sin and surrendering our will to Christ's. What might be a little more inconspicuous is the requirement to be newly changing as a result of each.

When we come to Christ, we are accepted as we are only in that very moment in which we seek forgiveness. Once we are forgiven, we are no longer the person we were just moments before, nor are we granted permission to remain as such. In doing so, we would remain in the same sinful state for which we just asked to be forgiven.

In forgiveness, we are a new person in Christ and with this newness comes the expectation that we be willing to learn to live as Jesus did. And in our willingness to learn, we exude our teachable capacity.

A hiring manager seeks this very same asset. As any manager is looking to fill a position, he posts a position vacancy. God, too, like the manager, is looking to fill open spots—open spots in the hearts of those who desire for Him to reside there. However, His posting never needs prior approval from management, never expires, no qualifications need to be met, no interview is necessary and as the vacancies are limitless, all are "hired."

Train

As good managers are drawn to and wisely invest in those who possess a questing appetite to learn as they are drawn towards success, God, too, is drawn to those whose hearts are driven toward success as their hearts yearn for God "teach me to do your will." Because God's greatest investment is His people, everything He has to offer will be given to match their driven efforts to live as Jesus did (See 1 John 2:6.)

Life would be grand if in seeking employment, secular job postings mirrored the one of Christ in that there are no qualifications to be met, as all are "hired." But if life were grand, we wouldn't be in search of *God's* job posting. It's quite a welcome relief and a humble acceptance to be loved and wanted by the King just as we are. It is an acceptance for which no worldly trade can compete.

How Are We Like the Applicant?

Just as a newly-hired employee chooses to move into a new title, Christians must be willing to move into the responsibilities of the granted title *Christian*. For some, this may be a brand-new title. If such is the case, this is the best time to begin to accept and fulfill the responsibilities that accompany such an honorary title. For others, the title was given so long ago, but one they've never taken ownership of.

We initiate the beginning of such ownership as we immerse ourselves in the diligent pursuit of living this title we possess in the hope that it will reward us with the spiritual growth that results from intimacy with Jesus, the joy that comes from the peace that God grants, the opportunity to be a servant unto Christ and the newness of life that results from the growth, joy and opportunity. In doing so, our valiant efforts will finally allow us to humbly take ownership of the royal title for which our hearts have quietly desired.

Why is the concept of responsibilities that accompany titles so easily understood and fulfilled when applied to all things secular? Any person who accepts a new job title knowingly accepts its concomitant responsibilities. But for some reason once we move from a secular title to a spiritual one, that same once-understood, grasped secular concept is lost spiritually. Perhaps this is attributable to our misunderstanding that we have *no* title responsibilities as Christians.

We long to be saved and as a result of our salvation, we are stamped as Christians. There comes expectancy with *any* new title—spiritual or secular. We receive a new title for a new journey, just as in the secular world. In order to receive all the growth, joy and opportunity from this new title, *we* must initiate the undertaking of our new responsibilities. It is only in fulfilling these responsibilities that we will blissfully live the newness of life afforded only by the growth, joy and opportunity presented.

The personal relationship with Jesus that we yearn for will aid our effort to emulate Him while living in obedience. In stepping into our new title of Christian, it is God's hope that we bring glory to Him while simultaneously stirring the lives of those around us that they too might long for the same ownership of such a dignified title. As we live for Jesus, we live His expectancies and as we live His expectancies, we live His will— "and he died for all, that those who live should no longer live for themselves but for him who died for them and was raised again" (2 Corinthians 5:15).

Some new titles are often accompanied by an increased monetary reward. In our new role as Christians, we too receive a reward, but not monetarily. Our reward is to one day hear God speak to us, "Well done, my good servant!" (Luke 19:17). These words divulge His approval of our choice to do His will, to live our responsibilities, to uphold our title. These words spoken by our Heavenly Father say to us, "I gladly approve of and take great pleasure in the life you have lived that served an honorable representation of My salvation." These words for us as Christians, should far outweigh any monetary recompense. We begin to realize there is no greater purpose in living than living for Christ.

As we are living faithfully and obediently to Him, we are striving towards: well done, good servant.

Train Yourself to Be Godly

Train yourself to be godly. For physical training is of some value, but godliness has value for all things, holding promise for both the present life and the life to come. – 1 Timothy 4:7-8

For some, the word *train* is laughable. These people do not hesitate to brazenly express that training, for them, is something in which they would never voluntarily choose to indulge. For others, the idea of training evokes a feeling of dread. The thought of investing the required time, the earnest perseverance and the unending effort is just too much for some to take on. Still yet, others have attempted to train and failed. Maybe at some point, they've allowed an uninvited defeatist mentality to consume their thoughts.

The word "train" is rarely associated with anything other than athletics. But when we broaden our understanding of "train" to include anything that we regard with high esteem, anything that is most meaningful to us or anything we feel is worth fighting for, then what possibly was once a negative interpretation of the word shifts to a much more positive interpretation.

Train

We train that we might remain—remain in all that we find incredibly valuable and extraordinarily dear to us. We train for our marriages, friendships, children, careers and even our homes. These are the things that we wholeheartedly and quite happily volunteer to dedicate our valuable time, earnest perseverance and unending effort because these are the things worth fighting (training) for that we might remain in them.

Do we, then, see our lives as Christians as meaningful, valuable and worth fighting for? Do we long to train that we might remain in a close, personal relationship with Jesus? Most likely we don't give much thought throughout the course of our days, if any, to the manifestation of our Christian life. I would like to think this is because we are already naturally living a Christian life, as expected.

So, in knowing how kind and loving the Father of our salvation is, wouldn't it seem logical then that *this* relationship would, above all others, take priority in our training? Training to be godly brings us only benefit; no one can train for us and no one can accept the responsibility, for us, that this training entails.

For those who grasp well the concept of "train" as it relates to athletics, let me make this analogy. In training to be godly, Christianity is the sport, the Holy Bible is the rule book and the goal is to live for Jesus. This spiritual training offers benefits that the physical training simply cannot: it doesn't necessitate a certain apparel, doesn't require us to drive in the busiest traffic to get to the training session, there is no nasty sweat with which to contend, and it's free! However, in *this* sport, we do not compete that others may lose. We train so that we, along with others, will be victorious.

This spiritual training requires commitment as any training requires commitment. But as our commitment to Jesus evolves into an ever closer and more loving relationship, we no longer see our training as drudgery. Now, we do it joyfully because we genuinely love more and more of Him in our lives.

Our training fills us with godly knowledge and wisdom. In applying these invaluable qualities to our lives, we are ever becoming Christlike not merely in pretense, but in our very heart and mind. We are slowly becoming new as we are becoming changed individuals. In order that we might remain this individual that we're ever becoming, we must ever train to be godly. At last, a daily *invited* training that we devotedly participate in that guarantees a transformation.

For Physical Training Is of *Some* Value

As discussed earlier in the chapter, the word "train" is laughable for some, while for others, it successfully summons dreadfulness. For those who do not take kindly to training for whatever reason, you'll be ecstatic to know that though God gives credence to physical training, He recommends only "some" physical training.

Although we cannot quantify "some," we can logically deduct that when compared to the godly training, the physical training is significantly less. As our goal is to emulate Christ, we conclude that the majority of the time we spend in training should be on the godly aspect. All the while, maintaining physical training.

Everyone concedes to the fact that physical training is incredibly beneficial to our health. Those who choose to exercise are not only those who are overweight, but also those who long to sustain a healthy weight and BMI. Regardless of the type and intensity of physical training we undertake, the results are noticeable not only in how we physically look, but also in how we physically feel. Ironically, physical training equips us with *more* energy. This unfamiliar, but much-welcomed abundance of energy is the desired relief required to offset our ever-growing to-do list.

In the article entitled, **Regular Exercise Changes the Brain to Improve Memory, Thinking Skills,** *it states,* *"Exercise changes the brain in ways that protect memory and thinking skills."*[3] The protection of both our memory and thinking skills is crucial to our godly training as it includes Scripture interpretation and memorization. As we meditate on memorized Scripture, our thinking skills allow for comprehension. Without grasping the *meaning* of the Scripture that's been committed to memory, there is no way for us to incorporate the imparted concept into our lives. Scripture must take on personal meaning and application, and the heart is where this happens. When the Word becomes personal, the manifestation of Christlike character is seen in how we live. Godly training yields Christlike character.

Take note of the very first word in the title of the article—regular. The placement of the word magnifies its lofty rank. Regularity is absolutely the most critical part of *any* training as it is what defines training. Regularity is the difference between cultivating an enduring marriage or one that succumbs to divorce. Daily training is the difference between those who choose to practice Christianity and those who choose to merely profess Christianity. In order to triumphantly maintain our godliness, our spiritual training must hinge on consistency. As regular physical training literally changes the brain, our regular godly training literally changes our mind and heart. Protected memory and thinking skills are priceless assets gained from regular physical training, which, in turn, only profit our spiritual training.

Train

At times, fighting to train regularly is an exhausting battle against both the enemy and the daily stresses of life. The enemy finagles his way into our minds to plant reasons to forego training for the day. We mustn't submit to his crafty seduction, for once leads to twice, and ultimately to a cessation of regular godly training.

But Godliness Has Value for All Things Holding Promise for Both the Present Life And the Life to Come

How frequently are promises spoken? How much more easily are they broken? Many people give seldom thought, if any, to the declaration made. Their word is given hastily, solely for their *own* advantage. It has become a selfish tactic whereby the receiver of the promise is often left expectantly waiting for its fulfillment. But when God makes a promise, He never breaks it—and His promises are never made for His own advantage. *Vine's Complete Expository Dictionary of Old and New Testament Words With Topical Index, Thomas Nelson, 1980, defines **promise** as "primarily a law term, denoting a summons," also meaning, "an undertaking to do or give something" (p. 491).* In today's society when one neglects to respond to a summons, one can potentially incur criminal penalties. Perhaps, we should treat promises (to do or give something) as they are summons hoping to influence more people to follow through in accomplishing their own promise. God, on the other hand, unfailingly upholds any and all promises He has made.

However, the receiving of some promises made by God are contingent upon some requirement being met by us before they are granted by Him. So, our part must be completed first before God carries out His part. For example, in Ephesians 6:2-3, before God grants the promise of a long life that will go well for us, we first must honor our father and our mother.

God doesn't promise that our part will be easy. Usually, our part will require a devoted and endless amount of time and unlimited effort. The choice to meet the requirement is ours.

It goes without saying then that as our obedience waxes and wanes, so do the promises of God. As we strive for obedience to become an involuntary response in our lives, God imparts His promises for both the present life and the life to come. While the apparent promise of the life to come is the promise of eternity, some of the promises for the present life include:

- Our barns will be filled with every kind of provision (Psalm 144:13).
- All hard work brings a profit (Proverbs 14:23).

- What the righteous desire will be granted (Proverbs 10:24).
- The Lord watches over all who love him (Psalm 145:20).

In a time when promises are spoken as often as we blink, yet fulfilled only as often as we enjoy going to work, and most advantageous to the promise maker and not the promise receiver, we run to God's promises. He preserves His declarations and in doing so draws us ever more nigh unto Him. His promises alone are all the encouragement ever needed to put forth our every effort toward godliness. As surely as we live obedience, He grants His promises with expedience.

We Teach Ourselves to Be Persistent

To those who by persistence in doing good seek glory, honor, and immortality, he will give eternal life. – Romans 2:7

Persistence isn't handed to us. We aren't born with it. We teach ourselves to be persistent. And we know that in seeking glory, honor and immortality this will be a most difficult labor, as Christ forewarns in His preface "to those who by *persistence*." The Scripture does not read, "to those in doing good seek glory, honor and immortality," which would suggest that doing good is an effortless task, almost as if the "doing good" part is something that automatically goes hand in hand with our salvation. But we, in our growing knowledge of God's Word, know all too well this is not the case. For those things worth having the most, require the most sacrifice and the most effort.

In doing good, we face daily—and I mean literally every single day—obstacles that require our know-how to hurdle. I personally cannot think of anything else that I've ever decided to live that has been met with such enormous opposition as my decision to live for Christ. In our desire to renovate our soul and move forward in all that is of God, one of the greatest oppositions we face is the spiritual battle with the enemy. For those who remain nonpaticipatory in their *Christian* lifestyle, which means the word Christian is something they lay claim to only in name and not in doing, the enemy remains haughtily complacent in the lives of those who have taken this route.

On the other hand, in his every effort to destroy our revived desire to actually live for Jesus in both truth and in deed, he forces upon us his expectant brawls. But, we abruptly and loudly shut down these brawls as we pull from our freshly stocked arsenal. We slash his haughty satisfaction with our songs of praise, and we paralyze his brawls as we recite God's Word.

His insatiable need for destruction motivates his incessant and unremitting attacks. His relentless attempts to make us weary, to force the waving of our white flag, to force our return to our nonpaticipatory Christian lifestyle have actually done the opposite—we are learning persistence!

This persistence is not reflective of our valiant fighting *perfection*. There will be days we feel downtrodden and void of the motivation needed to draw from the boldness and stoutheartedness with which God has equipped us to ward off the enemy's unremitting malice. But we will not allow ourselves to become alarmed. As we take our place on the battlefield, we will be there spiritually equipped and reenergized.

In our pursuit of glory, honor and immortality, we long to overcome the obstacles before us by implementing our practiced persistence. But at times, our minds become the playground where the enemy spends his time in laughter and scheming for days, months, years, even decades. As we allow our minds to become his playground, he swings our thoughts toward sin, traps us in tunnels of darkness where our lights are unable to shine, forces us to ride the teeter-totter of guilt and shame or worthlessness and depression. Finally, he pushes us down the slide that ends in mud and muck. And in this mud and muck, we struggle to simply stand and once we do, we allow ourselves to carry this grime for an indefinite amount of time as the mind is where we are either victorious or defeated.

As we help ourselves to own this persistence, God is sure to help us, even stepping in at times to fight the battle *for* us. We must *daily* prepare our weaponry for battle. We recharge our walkie batteries in praying daily. We fixate our walkie earpieces that we might clearly hear the essential guidance and revelation from the Holy Spirit. We stock our ammunition by loading and reloading our minds with memorized Scripture and as we strengthen our minds, we simultaneously strengthen our weaponry.

We must always remember in those times when we are faithless, He is faithful (See 2 Timothy 2:13.) We stand to gain the most priceless gift in all existence in our pursuit of glory, honor and immortality. This good is *not* works as some misinterpret, but the good we do is to please God in *all* things as we choose to live obediently. This gift made available only to those who by persistence live a life in doing good (See Romans 2:7.) This gift is eternity—we wave our checkered flag!

It Is a Matter of Mind Over Matter

I am of the opinion that the things most worth having are never easily obtained. If they were, everyone would have them. Persistence is one such quality most worth having—a quality that not everyone has pursued to possess. In the renovation of our souls, we learn that we cannot be victorious with a persistence that is only skin deep. As it dwells in that shallow surface, the struggle for survival is greatest as it wavers in its inception. But as we knit God's Word into the depths of our hearts thereby becoming a guide by which to live, persistence begins to take root. And although only skin deep at first, as we *live* God's precepts daily, those roots begin to burrow deeper and deeper.

The war waged in our minds, triggered by the enemy, is everlasting so it is imperative that we ever draw securely nearer to our Lord and Savior. The battles may become less frequent and less intense at times, but they are continual. Therefore, persistence is fundamental to our fight as we exercise mind over matter. When the enemy comes, he comes for no less than to kill, to steal and to destroy. Notice how these words are linked by the conjunction *and*. This means they *all* happen and they all happen simultaneously, each and every time we grant him a victory; one detriment cannot happen in and of itself. But in knowing *how* to defeat these thoughts, engaged only in persistence, the enemy must retreat. He has to retreat because just as light and darkness cannot occupy the same space at the same time, victory and defeat cannot be declared at the same time in the same battle. We make a choice regarding the lies of the enemy. We can choose to harbor them, thus allowing him to wreak havoc in our lives, or we can immediately seize them and speak the encouraging and promising Word of God to defeat them. We are victorious as we live mind over matter.

CHAPTER EIGHT

Evaluate

To successfully Evaluate, let us willingly eliminate.

To put it very simply, relationships either fail or endure. Those that endure are not always defined as successful. In order that they receive the stamp of success, joy must be the greatest attribute the relationship awards. But in choosing to endure, we have to first decide the worth of the relationship, maybe even the worth we ourselves feel within the relationship. We don't generally decide to endure any one situation or any one person unless we feel that there is something worthy to be gained. We understand that, more often than not, anything worth having in life is not easily obtained *or* maintained—but it is also true that anything worth having will bring us great joy.

Failed relationships are often due to a shortage of or even a complete absence of *regular* self-examination. Failed relationships are full of fault-finding, finger pointing and blame shaming on our significant other. Maybe we feel at times, the fault-finding is justifiable: perhaps infidelity was committed or a job offer declined because it wasn't enough pay even though it's almost been six months since being employed.

Sometimes in failing relationships, it's just easier to entertain the idea of starting over as joy is something which has been lacking for so long. We begin to reason that the excitement of something new must certainly bring joy. And we convince ourselves that change, something that's been long-awaited, is the remedy we need in order to procure this joy.

The bigger picture still remains to be seen, however. In choosing to abandon the present relationship and engage in a new one, sooner or later we find that the very same problems eventuate. Often times in deserting a relationship in hopes of finding a more promising one, we fail to realize that we ourselves contributed to that unsuccessful relationship in *some* way, whether big or small. At some point, hopefully, we come to the realization that we are the remaining constant in the succession of our multiple collapsed relationships.

Stamp of Success

What is success? The definition of success varies greatly regarding *what* we are actually attempting to define as

Evaluate

successful. And at that, it varies as greatly as the east is from the west or from person to person as it pertains to each individual life. But is there an underlying premise that all could agree upon in defining success?

Life offers very few situations in which most people can concede that success has been achieved. An acceptable consensus exists among most people that success has, in fact, been achieved when one lands a high-paying job, obtains a higher education, remains married to the same person until death and raises children who become productive members of society. But in all of these so-called achieved successes, did we ever consider whether any of these advancements yield joy.

Because we *quantify* success, we struggle to come to an across-the-board agreement of what success truly is. Most often, we quantify something by expressing it in numbers. As a result, we considerably narrow the scope of all that can accurately be defined as successful. In doing so, it is no wonder that relationships are not regarded as successful because they are not quantifiable in and of themselves. Nonetheless, the relationship *can* earn the stamp of success if the relationship bubbles with joy.

Remember, relationships can fail because of very infrequent or complete absence of regular self-examination (See Lamentations 3:40.) We fear that in examining ourselves, if we're honest, we will find that there is much-needed change, and most people oppose this change because it requires commitment, humility and time. The change that is most needed is not quantifiable because most likely the change required has much to do with our practiced character. This change includes areas like anger and forgiveness or pride and humility. And because we cannot quantify character, good or bad, it proves difficult to justify a relationship as successful. Most are simply not willing to put forth the effort that change requires so we choose to move on instead. Perhaps, if we'd chosen to stay long enough to implement the change then it's possible we would've reaped boundless reward.

Second Corinthians 4:18 tells us that which is seen is temporary, but that which is unseen is eternal. Although the change in practiced character is not physically seen, the manifestation of the changes made will eventually materialize. The benefits of change in areas that are unseen, if maintained, will reap lasting, eternal reward for believers. Any change that upholds a godly principal is good and most definitely worthy of the investment of our time. Relationships that are able to endure temporary upsets long enough to live the advantages of change will eventually yield the greatest attribute a relationship can produce. This is joy.

Any shortcomings or flaws that we've decided to change and have successfully implemented in our lives make us better people, but change that is accomplished within

Evaluate

believers will align with a godly characteristic. We press on in that change knowing that it is good and godly and because of this change, we are now better equipped to maintain any relationship.

We strive to acquire this same joyful relationship with our Heavenly Father. In order that it be accomplished, *regular* self-examination is necessary and the change needed must be met with unwavering, immovable, tenacious spirit. We are encouraged in this change when we don't allow ourselves to concentrate on our present flaws but instead choose to concentrate on the lifelong promises of a godly life lived aiming to please God.

The added benefit of changing for Christ is that we don't have to wait to profit joy. Christ never reminds us of where we used to be and who we once were. He is patient. He understands that change is a process, not an overnight stay at the local Holiday Inn Express. He continually loves us while we attempt to change. He is able to see us as the finished product. Even if we suddenly veer off course and briefly revert to our old self, Christ still loves us all the while, never finding fault or placing blame.

We long for both our secular relationships and our spiritual relationship with Jesus Christ to be joyous. Joy is our incentive to make the changes within ourselves that will enable the relationship to live on, perhaps even more joyfully than we ever thought possible. In attaining joy, we *have* achieved the stamp of success.

When the Going Gets Rough, We Get Going

"Some things never change." We're all guilty of having made that statement too many times to count—often out of anger and frustration. But why is it that some things never change? It is simply because some people never change.

In our finite thinking as humans, we resolve to start over when we feel that our relationship is not all it's cracked up to be. Starting over, by far, is the most sought-after choice of escape from relationships that once cheerfully absorbed us. At the beginning of that relationship, all we could think about was the newness of how that person made us feel, that as we loved, a love was happily returned, and how we longed for the warm embrace of one another that seemed to bring healing at the end of a long, strenuous day.

These are the very same reasons we once made a vow to remain in the relationship, to promise to do all we possibly could to ensure it remained unbroken. But for whatever reason, the relationship began to sour and we began to feel as if resolution was hopeless. So, we arrived at the conclusion that it's not all it's cracked up to be. We ultimately decide that, when the going gets rough, we get going.

Evaluate

Has this become our default mindset? Has our thinking become warped somehow into believing that we've taken the high road because we feel it would be less condemning and more logical not to cause further undue tension, anxiety and stress—which is felt by everyone who is part of or exposed to that relationship? It seems so, as is evidenced by the number of children that come from broken homes and blended families.

And unfortunately, it isn't just marital relationships that we're choosing to abandon. In all sorts of life relationships and even our spiritual relationship with Christ—when the going gets rough, we get going.

Consider the job that you finally landed that would impart the necessary instruction in specific skills and grant the significant people associations needed that would help lead to advancement. After months of training in this new position, a coworker continued to cause problems. You quit the job.

Your son made the varsity football team as a sophomore. The hours he spent daily in the gym and on the field were recognized. The coach that promoted him to varsity decided to take another coaching position at a different high school. Your son couldn't get along with the new coach. He quit football.

You've consistently made payments on a new car purchase, but your hours at work were unexpectedly and considerably cut back. You did not attempt to find a second job to make up for the lost hours or perhaps a better paying job altogether. You allowed the car to be repossessed.

You've lived a life of obedience since being saved. You began intermingling with those you thought you *might* be able to encourage living a life unto Jesus. Rather, *you* began to dabble in the same sin they were living. You carried the burden of guilt instead of seeking forgiveness and change. You abandoned your relationship with Jesus.

When the going gets rough, we get going.

The Million $ Question

Essentially, every choice, every single choice we will ever make in the course of our lifetime boils down to one single million-dollar question: is it worth it?

Is it worth having left the job you knew would aid in promotion? Is it worth having quit the sport you love and your desire for competition that drove you to spend countless hours training both physically and mentally? Is it worth having allowed your guaranteed transportation to be repossessed only now to tackle the questionable reliance of a buddy or the transit system to get you everywhere you need to be? Is it worth having lost a friend that sticks closer than a brother (See Proverbs 18:24) and a life of eternity with Him?

Evaluate

Who determines whether it's worth it? We do, of course. Are we evaluating the worth of the situation itself or the worth we ourselves feel within the situation? It is a far better plan to choose the worth we ourselves feel within the situation.

The problem in trying to assess the worth of the situation itself is that we automatically begin to focus solely on the person or people, whom we believe, are causing for us the tumultuous uproar in our lives. Therein lies the difficulty; our inability to separate the assets the situation may bestow from the abundance of drawbacks brought forth by our conflict with others.

We can only, with absolutely no distractions, efficaciously evaluate the worth of the situation. Most ordinarily, though unrealistic, with no distractions to mislead us or cause disruption in our thought process, we can arrive at valid conclusions that allow us to determine whether the situation is worthwhile or not. We can conclude that the job would afford us the opportunity for advancement, the additional hours we work would serve to keep us from being idle while earning enough money to keep our transportation, in remaining married we're not forced to partake in the limited weekly visits to see our very own children, and lastly, we spend an eternity with Jesus Christ.

Figuring Ourselves Out

It is a far better plan to choose the worth we ourselves feel within any given situation—which is healthy rather than selfish. Regular self-examination helps us begin to realize how we truly feel about ourselves in our identity as Christians. Self-examination will either confirm an ongoing growth in our Christlike character or a stagnation of it. We finally begin to figure ourselves out, but only with the guidance of the Holy Spirit. As the self-examination process begins, we may already really like who we are. We awaken each morning with a clear conscience. We may already possess great joy and attribute our joy to our salvation, but we acknowledge the hard-core truth that we can stand to be more like Jesus.

Or we may awaken each morning without even knowing we are guilty of leading a stagnant Christian life. For example, we may concede to owning feelings of lust. However, in our current relationship, we honestly feel we have been devoted and fully committed even though we spend a considerable amount of time daydreaming and fantasizing about being with someone else. We justifiably reason that because we've never *physically* acted upon our thoughts, all is well. In choosing to lead a life devoid of Christ, we force ourselves to become stagnant. Little do

Evaluate

we know that entertaining these thoughts, however briefly or infrequently, will inevitably lead to sin of some kind, in some way. It may even be the culprit for our struggling relationship. But only as a result of wanting to change and incorporating self-examination, do we finally realize we've been stagnant in living and growing Christlike character.

Regardless of the current state of mind during self-examination, *every single person* can afford change or modification in some aspect of one's life. We may finally admit a change is long overdue, but pinpointing where the rework is needed can sometimes be difficult. Sometimes, it simply may be that the desired change is merely an expansion or maturation in some aspect of our life that we currently exercise. For example, we may find forgiveness to be effortless for those whom we care about or for those whom we love deeply, while laboring to forgive those whom we are not particularly close to or toward whom we feel indifference. Advancement and development in this domain will certainly allow us to draw ever nearer to Christ the King in our relationship with Him because we honed in on the expansion and growth of godly character.

On the other hand, there are those that are fully cognizant of the fact that the life they lead in no way emulates Christ, thus forcing the awareness of much-needed change in a variety of manners. They do not petition that change because of the overwhelming amount needed. Perhaps they are underestimating, even though they're saved, the power of God who aids substantially in the process of reformation. They conclude, I am who I am.

I Am Who I Am

It is during this self-examination that we can sometimes discover that we are responsible for settling with the self-imposed, defeatist mentality—I am who I am. And in doing so, we somehow negate our very own worthiness. Because we possess very little or no self-worth, we tend to view ourselves as having the least to offer while ignoring that we've already gained the most. We did so in choosing to become a child of the King—the King of all kings, at that. We are descendants of royalty. We inherited the power to accomplish and to take hold of all that we thought was unattainable and unreachable, a lie from the enemy to destroy our relationships. We compared ourselves to others and thought, *Why does it happen for others and not me?* It is, in fact, because we believed the lie that we have no worth. In believing that lie, we held onto it, thus prohibiting us from stepping out in faith to begin change.

This power that we inherited lies in the blood. It is so powerful that it removed our transgressions and gave us promise of eternal life. The cross has prevailed. The

Evaluate

blood that Jesus shed is the outward trophy—the outward understanding of eternal promise for those who believe in Jesus Christ and believe that God raised Him from the dead. This is power that we must recognize and utilize—power that resulted from the sacrificial atonement for our sins. This sacrifice for us, a sinful people, is the starting point upon which self-worth is generated as the very God of heaven and earth validated our worth in the death of His only Son.

In confessing the above, we can step out in faith to begin the process of the change that is needed in us to mend relationships and then give praise to God for having been granted the gift of time—a welcomed opportunity to implement the change. In becoming more and more the emulation of Christ by the Holy Spirit, it is then that we acknowledge our worthiness and this worthiness will catapult us into the desire to begin the change sought. The Bible says in Luke 12:6 and 7:

> *Are not five sparrows sold for two pennies?*
> *Yet not one of them is forgotten by God.*
> *Indeed, the very hairs of your head are all numbered.*
> *Don't be afraid; you are worth more than many sparrows.*

Can you imagine attempting to count the hairs on your head? God is specific. He pays attention to detail. He gives detail to everything and in this detail, He knows that *He* possesses it. This detail makes it one of a kind, set apart from all others, in a class all its own—given and blessed by Him. The detail given by God gives it its beauty and *worth*. So even if we have no hair on our head, God has given and blessed us with something that is exclusive to each of us. We can rest assured that no one, absolutely no one, has what we alone have.

We are so worthy in His eyes that each person is set apart from others and in a class all his own. Claim that self-worth in the name of Jesus. Take hold of it. Retain it. So whether a thought is generated in our minds to negate our self-worth or someone cruelly speaks an attack against our self-worth, immediately seize it and reject it.

Each and every time we hear such an utterance, we must purposely follow it up with a positive and encouraging Scripture to combat the negative. But we must be diligent and unfailing in combatting the negative, debasing comments with uplifting, edifying statements. If not, we ultimately allow ourselves to begin again the battle to claim our self-worth. We revert once again to the conclusion—*I am who I am.*

We can be so much more in Christ Jesus. We truly can be. In making the choice to live a changed life daily by the renovating of our soul, our lives finally serve as proof that reformation leads to transformation.

EndNotes

1. https://en.wikipedia.org/wiki/Peripheral_vision
2. http://www.mayoclinic.org/tests-procedures/marriage-counseling/basics/definition/PRC-20012741
3. http://www.health.harvard.edu/blog/regular-exercise-changes-brain-improve-memory-thinking-skills-201404097110

www.ingramcontent.com/pod-product-compliance
Lightning Source LLC
Chambersburg PA
CBHW060354080526
44583CB00012B/306